CW01081194

ZODIAC

MONMOUTHSHIRE

Edited by Steve Twelvetree

First published in Great Britain in 2002 by
YOUNG WRITERS
Remus House,
Coltsfoot Drive,
Peterborough, PE2 9JX
Telephone (01733) 890066

HB ISBN 0 75433 700 6
SB ISBN 0 75433 701 4

FOREWORD

Young Writers was established in 1991 with the aim of promoting creative writing in children, to make reading and writing poetry fun.

Once again, this year proved to be a tremendous success with over 41,000 entries received nationwide.

The Zodiac competition has shown us the high standard of work and effort that children are capable of today. The competition has given us a vivid insight into the thoughts and experiences of today's younger generation. It is a reflection of the enthusiasm and creativity that teachers have injected into their pupils, and it shines clearly within this anthology.

The task of selecting poems was a difficult one, but nevertheless, an enjoyable experience. We hope you are as pleased with the final selection in *Zodiac Monmouthshire* as we are.

CONTENTS

Sarah Jane Stokes 21
Lindsey Keren Bidgway 22
Kyle Butler 22
Martyn Fortune 23
Ross Gardiner 23
Sarah Bettell-Higgins 24
Sinéad Brennan 24
Laura Yip 25
Sara Wright 25
Philip Thomas 25
Daniel Russell 26
Tanya Mellens 26
Jason Williams 27
Jodie Lee Shankland 27
Hannah Spillett 28
Kerys Williams 28
Matthew Rees 29
Vicki Pugh 29
Rhodri Isaacs 30
Emma Perry 30
Amy Lee King 31
Natalie Marie Lucas 31
Sara Edwards 32
Aimee Meredith 32
Siän Louise Fuller 33
Kayleigh Bidgway 34
Ben Rowberry 34
Carly Jade Watkins 35
Rhian Gamlin 35
Ieuan Wall 36
Ross Lewis Forbes 36
Katie Reynolds 37
Claire Gwilt 37
Mark Evans 38
Michael John Carey 38
Aaron Williams 39
Siân Haynes 39
Daniel Jefferies 40

Rachel Knight	60
Kirsty Yemm	61
Gareth James	61
Giselle Quarrington	62
Gareth Roberts	62
Rhiannon Wells	63
Tom Vaughan	63
Patrick O'Malley	64
Katie Edmondson	64
Kate Hanbury	65
Charlotte Morris	66
Kelan Handley	66
Michaela Williams	67
Natasha Matthews	68
Geraint Hatherall	68
Rhys Davies	69
Nicola Morris	70
Laura Copeland	71
Laura Powell	72
Sam Collins	72
Craig Matthews	73
Rachel James	73
Jodie Malnati	74
Tom Roberts	74
Robert Pritchard	75
Christy Collings	75
Beth Kelly	76
Rhian Auty	76
Roxanne Generalovic	77
Neil Powell	78
Emma Davies	79
Priya Mohan	80
Kashanie Tye	80
Sarah Holder	81
Amy Trinder	82
Robert Powell	83
Becky Cochrane	84
Kayleigh Down	84

Lewis Davies	85
Laura Davies	85
Jack Morse	86
David Bishop	86
Emily Williams	86
Natasha Williams	87
Nesta Watkins	87
Rosie Powell	88
Kate Jones	88
Hannah Burch	89
Adele Morgan	90
Nathan Byrne	90
Mari Davies	91
Hannah Goldsworthy	92
Eleanor Roberts	92
Kate Miles	93
Elin Jones	93
Helena Nilsson	94
Sarah Dobbins	94
Katie McCarthy	95
Arwyn Woodford	95
Katie Lias	96
Rachel Gooding	96
Chloe Williams	97
Kimberly Jones	97

Monmouth Comprehensive School

Rachael Hughes	98
Sara Garrett	98
Claire Tremlett	99
Chloe West	99
Tom Garwood	100
Michaela Painter	100
Mathew Willcock	101
Katie Small	101
Rebecca Couchman	102
Joe Waters	102
Amy Phillips	103

The Poems

THE PLANETS

Nine planets there are,
Large ones and small ones
And a sideways one too!
Earth, Jupiter, Uranus, Pluto,
Mercury, Saturn and the blue Neptune
And of course Mars and Venus,
You must not forget!
Those last two are closest to us,
The two biggest are Saturn and Jupiter.
So my poem's come to an end
And I hope you remember,
Nine planets there are
With nine different names.

Joanne Gould (13)
Blackwood Comprehensive School

SCHOOL

School will start at 8.30,
My first subject is geography.
Mr Jones starts to talk,
The children think he's a joke.
Ring ring the bell will go,
We all run out then fall on the floor.
By the time dinner comes
Everyone gets ready to run,
So they all run out like some fools.
When it's time to line up no one's there,
The teachers say well we don't care,
So they all drive home in pairs.

Emma Heath (12)
Blackwood Comprehensive School

A LITTLE LOST DOG

A little lost dog that wanders the street,
A little lost dog wondering who he shall meet,
A little lost dog looking for food,
A little lost dog in a sad, sad mood.

No one to love him,
No one to care.

A little lost dog getting cold as in creeps night air,
A little lost dog with nowhere to go,
A little lost dog sad and alone,
A little lost dog which hasn't a bed.

But who is on the bench by where he sits,
A little girl who looks sad and forlorn,

A little lost dog now has a home.

Jade Williams (12)
Blackwood Comprehensive School

THE ZODIAC

The zodiac has an affect on our lives,
It casts a shadow on every man, woman and child,
The planets all link like a long, colourful chain,
Though some people think it is all a real pain.
Everyone owns their own special sign
Depending on when they were born,
There are twelve signs for each month
So nobody won't be without one at all.
One day you might be rich but for now you'll be poor,
Just look up at the stars and pray that one day you'll have it all.

Kristina Jones (12)
Blackwood Comprehensive School

VICTOR SPOON'S TRIP TO THE MOON!

There was a man named Victor Spoon,
Who jumped in a rocket and flew to the moon.
As he gazed into the sky,
He stared at the stars that twinkled nearby.

'Ten seconds to go, I'll be there soon,'
Then with a bump he landed on the moon.
Next he noticed something weird,
Three four-eyed aliens with ten legs and a beard!

They walked towards him starting to chase,
They had purple lumps all over their face.
They started shooting revolting green slime,
Victor just wished he could stop time.

Suddenly he was inside his rocket,
The disgusting slime oozed from his pocket.
'This can't be the moon,' he said 'can it?'
'Oops, I've landed on Mars the planet!'

Ellen Rowe (12)
Blackwood Comprehensive School

ASTROLOGY

A ries is the first sign
S corpio and Sagittarius
T hey are two more
R arely does a day
O r week go by when I
L ook to see if my luck is in.
O ccasionally I am
G oing to win the Lottery apparently.
Y ou'll never believe it, neither do I!

Grant John Edwards (12)
Blackwood Comprehensive School

ZODIAC SIGNS

I'm an Aries, what are you?
My zodiac pals are independent, energetic and say what they think too!
My sign belongs to the fire group, including Leo and Sagittarius
                                                    as well,
You might be in the group Water, Air or Earth, but I could never tell!
But your horoscopes could tell, telling your fortune is their job,
Your horoscope will fill you in on your future, no prob.
The position of the planets is always changing,
And the places of the stars, are always rearranging.
This mysterious thing happens, to show people's forecast,
One week it's all the gossip, the next it's all in the past.
You may read about love, life and laughs or perhaps your bad
                                                    and lucky days,
Or maybe you don't believe in all this, and avoid these
                                            superstitious ways.
Virgo, Pisces, Aries and Taurus, Gemini, Cancer and there's
                                            more of us,
Libra, Scorpio and Sagittarius and finally Capricorn and Aquarius.
These are all the zodiac signs, you could be falling in love,
                                    or falling out with a mate,
But whatever they say about you, they all do the same, and that's
                                    reveal your mystical fate!

Sarah Rogers (12)
Blackwood Comprehensive School

WAR

War is horrid war is bad,
Some people were in the Army aged only a lad.
With air bombs, artillery, tanks and more,
You'd better watch out, explosions galore!

Hitler was a psycho some people say,
But he could be a hero in another sort of way.
Many battles were fought, lost and won,
But remember many people died by a bullet from a gun.

Matthew Phillpott (12)
Blackwood Comprehensive School

RIDDLES OF THE ZODIAC

I am a well known star sign,
My clippers are very sharp.
I am a small, black creature
Who usually feeds in the dark
What am I?

I tolerate the moon and stars,
I despise the sun.
When you shine a torch on me,
I turn away and run
What am I?

I'm a well known figure in space,
Twirling round and round.
If I accidentally swallow you up,
I'm sure you'll never be found.
What am I?

I am a big, bright sphere,
The brightest sphere in space.
I am used as an energy source,
And put a smile on your face.
What am I?

Ross Duggan (14)
Blackwood Comprehensive School

THE NIGHT SKY'S SHOOTING STARS

As I look to the stars above,
They glisten in the moonlight.
The twinkling stars change colour
Silver, gold, yellow and white.

The twinkling jewels
Float in the velvet night.
The rockets zoom past,
While they sit, shiny and bright.

I wish I could see them close up,
But I'd be happy here,
Watching the star signs,
Taurus, Virgo and Leo shining in the night.

Tomorrow I will see them again,
Up there, shining in the night.
The twinkling stars change colour,
Silver, gold, yellow and white.

Marco Carpanini (11)
Blackwood Comprehensive School

AUTUMN DAYS

Misty mornings, dark nights,
Leaves are changing overnight,
Red, yellow, orange and brown,
All lying on the ground.
Crickety, crackety conkers
Smashing and crashing
Into one.

Rebecca McDonald (12)
Blackwood Comprehensive School

LEAVING HOME

I have to admit it's strange,
Not having a big brother around,
The telephone seems to have stopped ringing,
Favourite crisps are easily found,

The washing line looks strange,
His trendy clothes have gone,
No one left to argue with,
Now that my brother's moved on!

It's strange with no one at the computer,
The table laid for three not four,
I wonder what he's doing now
'Oh' what a coincidence, he's walking through the door.

Gemma Aubrey (12)
Blackwood Comprehensive School

ZODIAC

The zodiac is a wondrous place with stars that shine so bright.
They shine through the darkness of the night and spread their
                                                heavenly light.
They guide our sailors on the seas to fetch them home to
                                                their families.
We take our birth signs from the stars such as Leo, Libra
                                                and Sagittarius.
The constellation that I see seems to paint pictures just for me.
The crystals in the dark, dark sky are roadways to the Milky Way.
They sparkle and glisten and shoot away
And I wake up to a brand new day.

Scott Anthony Marshall (11)
Blackwood Comprehensive School

STAR GAZING

Capricorn, the fish-tailed goat
Is determined and efficient.
Aquarius, the water bearer,
Is charming and altruistic.

Pisces, the fish
Is sensitive and tolerant.
Aries, the ram
Is courageous and trusting.

Taurus, the bull
Is peaceful and gentle.
Gemini, the twins
Is curious and versatile.

Cancer, the crab
Is ambitious and loyal.
Leo, the lion
Is enthusiastic and joyous.

Virgo, the virgin
Is helpful and organised.
Libra, the scales
Is diplomatic and rational.

Scorpio, the scorpion
Is strong and patient.
Sagittarius, the archer
Is honest and lucky.

All twelve signs of the zodiac have different shapes and stars
Do you know what you are?

Karina Emma Young (11)
Blackwood Comprehensive School

THE ZODIAC

Capricorn, the sign of the goat
For many years you have inspired folk

Aquarius, the sign of the water carrier
Smile to yourself as you realise both you and your conscious
are on the same side

Pisces, the sign of the fish
Even in the threat of danger Pisces will owe you a wager

Aries, the sign of the ram
Always trying to give a helping hand

Taurus, the sign of the bull
Strong and bold, too strong to hold

Gemini, the sign of the twins
The same, but different in every way

Cancer, the sign of the crab
Like the crab snappy and angry

Leo, the sign of the lion
Always braver than many by far

Virgo, the sign of the virgin
The purest person you'll ever meet

Libra, the sign of the weighing scales
Weighs up his problems and makes the right choice

Scorpio, the sign of the scorpion
Their sting is worse than their bite

Sagittarius, the last sign of the zodiac, last but not least.

Lloyd Hambridge (12)
Blackwood Comprehensive School

ZODIAC

There are loads of signs for zodiac,
Like Leo, Pisces and many more.
Everyone has a star sign of their own,
Even the president of the USA!

I don't normally remember my star sign,
I think it's . . . or maybe it's . . . oh I remember
It's . . . ugh . . . Leo!

I never bother reading my horoscope,
In The Sun or The Daily Telegraph,
They're never right anyway,
They say 'Great riches will come your way,'
But my allowance was cut down to £2.00
A week!

So zodiac is just suns and planets,
And the horoscopes aren't always right,
But it's something to believe in.

Aries is the ram in the sky,
The giver of money,
The protector of all.

Taurus is the bull of contest,
He fights in all games,
Causes havoc wherever he goes,
But he's only trying to have some fun.

Gemini tries daring new challenges,
Leading you home when you are lost,
Never leaving you alone
And leading you to safety when you are in grave danger.

There are loads more star signs,
Too many for me to explain,
But in the end you just can't believe
That they're a load of mumbo-jumbo!

Frank Rolls (12)
Blackwood Comprehensive School

THE YOB

A piece of Mars fell on my head,
While I was chewing on my bread.
This piece of rock was as big as my fist,
Now my head was a bit of a mist.
This piece of rock caused me pain,
While I was picking at my brain.
This piece of rock was red as blood,
It gave me a bit of a shud.
This piece of rock looked like a ball,
It sprouted legs and started to crawl.
His legs were green as slimy snobs,
He looked like a bit of a yob.
The yob went up the road,
I don't think it knew the Highway Code.
This little yob started to grow,
This yob was as big as a tree,
Then I found the yob was a she.
I wanted to keep her as a pet,
I won't tell Mum quite yet.

Nathan Hurley (12)
Blackwood Comprehensive School

THE SKY

The sky is a pretty place,
Stars glowing out of space.
As you look up into the sky,
You almost think you can fly.
Flying through the air so fast,
You don't even know that time has passed.

When you look at the dazzling stars,
It hurts so much you think it'll leave scars.
When you zoom past the planet Mars,
You can see aliens fighting with bars.
When you bump into four-eyed monsters,
All you wish is that you're back on Earth.
When you know you're back on Earth,
You realise it wasn't so bad.
After all it could've been worse.

Keith Davies (12)
Blackwood Comprehensive School

LOVELY LIBRA

Lovely, loopy Librans are the best.
I guess you know they're never a pest,
Librans can be charming and delightful,
But sometimes the boys can be rather frightful.
Other star signs sometimes whine,
While my star sign always shines
Like a gleaming star in the sky.
People stop and say I wish your star sign
Could be mine!

Amanda Summers (13)
Blackwood Comprehensive School

STAR SIGNS

There are twelve signs of the zodiac
For every month of the year.
They are for everyone's birthday
Which offer you doom, gloom and cheer.
The first is for Aries
This is the sign of the ram,
The second is for Taurus
These are for Feb and for Jan.
Gemini is after the bull
This is the sign of the twins,
My birthday comes next
It is Cancer
This is when summer begins,
The sign is for people who are born
In the month of July
This is when I was born
And the crab is my star sign.
Leo is next
It's the sign of the lion,
Followed by Virgo
And Libra, the sign of the scales,
Scorpio is the sign of the scorpion
With a nasty sting in its tail.
Next comes Sagittarius
Half man and half horse,
Followed by Capricorn and Aquarius
Followed by Pisces, of course
Everyone has a star sign,
But I like mine the most.

Abbie Louize Matthews (12)
Blackwood Comprehensive School

SIGNS OF THE ZODIAC

Aries, the ram is full of energy,
Who easily loses their temper and wants things to happen immediately.
Taurus, the bull is a good-natured sort,
They love to keep fit, but can be very stubborn.
Gemini, the twins are always in two minds,
They're bright and quick, but tell fibs and pull tricks.
Cancer, the crab is sensitive and thoughtful,
They love helping in the kitchen and really take things to heart.
Leo, the lion is courageous and proud,
But they're too cocky for their own good sometimes and show-off.
Virgo, the virgin is practical and clever,
They're always worrying and aim for perfection.
Libra, the scales is tolerant, but also lazy,
They're mega persuasive and like to cheer people up.
Scorpio, the scorpion is mysterious and strong-willed,
They're great swimmers and divers and love ghost stories.
Sagittarius, the archer always looks on the bright side,
They tend to exaggerate and are full of enthusiasm.
Capricorn, the goat likes to take life seriously,
They're ambitious and willing to work.
Aquarius, the water carrier is independent,
They need to feel free to be happy and at ease.
Pisces, the fish has a heart of gold,
They're daydreamers and often bite off more than they can chew.
Aries, Leo and Sagittarius are the Fire signs and burst with energy.
Taurus, Virgo and Capricorn are the Earth signs with common sense.
Gemini, Libra and Aquarius are the Air signs and are full of ideas.
Cancer, Scorpio and Pisces are the Water signs who brim with emotion.
There are twelve planets in the sky,
Each has a star sign belonging to it.

Sarah Blackwell (12)
Blackwood Comprehensive School

STARGAZING

Every evening through my window
I look with wondrous eye
At all the stars and planets
Scattered in the sky.

Each star I am counting
Each like a little sum
And the sky is really pretty
With all her lights left on.

If I stare too hard
The stars will swim in my eyes
Drifting towards my bedroom
Down the big sloping skies.

How odd it is that certain stars
Whose lights now still glow
Vanished from the sky
Three million years ago.

Amy-Leigh Faircloth (12)
Blackwood Comprehensive School

CLOTHES

C an't get enough of them
L ove the fashions and new styles
O ut, out, out I could walk for miles
T en pounds, twenty pounds, I don't care how much
H ope my dad continues to be a soft touch
E tam, Tammy, I shop in them all
S o I have to keep buying because I'm getting so tall.

Harriet Lewis (12)
Blackwood Comprehensive School

A Shire Horse

I love to see a shire horse,
Toiling through the day,
Working for the farmer
In his own sweet, willing way.
His eyes are liquid dark,
His coat is dappled grey,
His mane and tail remind me
Of a snowy winter's day.
He pulls the plough in winter
Then helps to make the hay,
And sometimes in the summer
He pulls the brewer's dray.
And in his stable, snug and warm,
At the closing of each day,
He stays until another dawn,
And eats his fill of oats and hay.

Abbie Murphy (13)
Blackwood Comprehensive School

The Road

T he road is a very dangerous place.
H igh speed chases are often made.
E very day people get killed.

R oad racers, just speeding away.
O vertaking whatever is in their way
A nd then they hit another car. Then
D ead is what they are in the end.

Alun Davies (12)
Blackwood Comprehensive School

THE ZODIAC

The zodiac consists of twelve star signs
These are depicted in the following lines
Large, curly horns on the head are grown
On the figure of a ram by which Aries is known.
Curved horns adorn Taurus the bull
And with Gemini twins your life would be full
Does Cancer the crab walk sideways on?
Followed by majestic Leo, the brave lion.
And if Virgo, the woman, ever fails
To catch the eye of Libra holding his scales
She could always look out for Scorpio the scorpion
Who's being preyed on by Sagittarius the archer
And is it correct that all Capricorns were born
Under the sign of the goat's horns?
And is Aquarius the water carrier aware
That the fishes of Pisces are in the water there?
Will the answer to these questions ever unfold
When the zodiac has been a mystery since times of old?

Stacey Dix (13)
Blackwood Comprehensive School

ZODIAC

Z   ooming stars across the night sky
O   range moon flying by
D   ark sky glistening high
I   cy winds blowing by
A   stronauts hovering in space
C   an you believe it? Neither can I.

Alex Organ (11)
Blackwood Comprehensive School

ZODIAC

Among all the comets and shooting stars,
we have the planets, Venus, Earth and Mars.
Are there such things as UFOs?
Nobody knows!
Sagittarius is the horoscope for me,
but you can also get Virgo, Gemini and Pisces.
The North Star and Milky Way
are billions of miles away.
Man has been to the moon,
but are hoping to go further real soon.
If you went up into space today,
it would be so peaceful,
you'd wish you could stay!

Katie Bracegirdle (13)
Blackwood Comprehensive School

THE ZODIAC

Stars and planets orbit and swirl through the vast black wasteland,
Constellations sparkle like diamonds in the black space that
                                    surrounds them,
Some say the future can be predicted by the zodiac,
Your star signs can tell you what will happen they say,
There are Aries, Scorpio, Virgo and many more,
Shooting stars fly across the sky and the moon glows as these rocks
                                    enter our harsh atmosphere.
The zodiac's intriguing beauty and complexity can be enjoyed by all,
By peering at the dark night sky.

Jon Maguire (12)
Blackwood Comprehensive School

ZODIAC

The zodiac, far, far away,
Floating by the Milky Way,
So far away I cannot say,
For the clouds are in the way.

The future, your destiny can be seen,
Check out your star sign,
All will be revealed,
The zodiac,
The planets,
All different signs,
Aries the ram, that one is mine.

The rest can be seen,
But don't believe,
All that you see,
For they could be,
Just some fantasy!

Darren Hiscox (13)
Blackwood Comprehensive School

ZODIAC SIGNS

Twelve plants in the sky, one of them belong to I,
The one that does is called Sagittarius, not Aries or Aquarius.
The other planets that still remain are still waiting to be claimed.
Astrology is a wonderful thing that tells people important things.
Gems and rocks show the way, but dates of birth are here to stay.
Zodiac signs tell you a story on Cancer, Capricorn, Scorpio and Pisces.
Leo is a lion, Taurus is a bull, in a different world one becomes all.
Libra, Virgo and Gemini are similar things as they all involve people
and their lives!

Siobhan Brajer (12)
Blackwood Comprehensive School

THE ZODIAC

If you're Virgo, Libra or Scorpio,
There is something you should know,
You're gonna' be big and flash,
'Cause soon you'll be rolling in lots of cash.

Sagittarius, Capricorn and Aquarius are next,
Here is something you won't expect,
Your future is planned and set,
But soon you'll be falling into debt.

Pisces, Aries and Taurus the bull,
You've been finding life very dull,
But don't be glum, come on you'll see,
There's lots of hope for your family.

Gemini, Cancer and Leo as well,
Your new job isn't going very well,
You don't know how you're going to cope,
Find out in next week's horoscope.

Robert Holdroyd (14)
Blackwood Comprehensive School

THE ZODIAC

Spread across the darkness of space,
Aries the ram battles Taurus the bull,
A battle of strength and horns,
But Leo roars out and startles the bull.

Libra holds the twins in balance,
Until Cancer tips the scales,
A comet sparkling across the night sky,
Looks like an arrow from Sagittarius' bow.

Aquarius stares down through a sea of stars,
At Pisces who swims through galaxies,
Virgo sparkles in the night sky,
Whilst Capricorn leaps over the scorpion with joy.

Christopher Evans (13)
Blackwood Comprehensive School

I HAVE NO INSPIRATION

I have no inspiration to write books about planes and cars
And stories about people, places and even planets afar.

I have no inspiration to write letters to family or friends
About what I do from day to day or people I meet,
Where can this end?

I have no inspiration to write a poem that rhymes like
I've just done . . .

Mark Bennett (13)
Blackwood Comprehensive School

ZODIAC

Z   ooming through space in a spaceship
O   bserve the stars twinkling in the sky
D   eep outer space
I   lluminous stars shine in space
A   tmosphere is a wonderful world
C   omets shooting through the night sky.

Sarah Jane Stokes (13)
Blackwood Comprehensive School

A FRIEND

A friend is forever,
A friend is for life,
Never let them go,
Or you'll be thinking twice.

If someone else come along,
Keep your friendship safe and strong,
You'll never be alone
When your friend is around,
You'll feel right at home,
With your feet firmly on the ground.

So just remember all your life,
A friend is forever,
This chance may not come twice.

Lindsey Keren Bidgway (12)
Blackwood Comprehensive School

ZODIAC POEM

Look at the stars that shine so bright,
In the clear sky at night,
Gemini, Virgo, Sagittarius,
Cancer, Leo and Aquarius.
Signs tell you who you are
At the same time, quite a laugh
In the newspapers they're advertised,
But mostly they're a bunch of lies.
Stars are interesting in how they look,
I even read so in a book
I like stars in different ways.
I sit on my bed for hours and gaze.

Kyle Butler (12)
Blackwood Comprehensive School

THE ZODIAC

Capricorn, the mystical goat of the distant space,
Aquarius, the gleaming water carrier of the outlying infinity,
Pisces, the awe-inspiring fish in the ocean of space,
Aries, the commanding ram of the far blue yonder,
Taurus, the overpowering bull dominating the night sky,
Gemini, the twins that stargazers observe with wonder,
Cancer, the mysterious crab which scuttles across the
                                        shores of the universe,
Leo, the mighty lion that rules the expanse of the galaxies
                                        of our universe,
Virgo, the virgin which is full of mystery,
Libra, the weighing scales of entirety,
Sagittarius, the skilled archer that fires shooting stars from its bow,
Scorpio, the scorpion that fills superstitious stargazers with amazement.

Martyn Fortune (13)
Blackwood Comprehensive School

ASTROLOGY

A strology means to study the stars.
S earching for an answer.
T omorrow's actions you can see.
R eal or not, it's up to you.
O nly you can act upon the answer.
L ots of different signs to see.
O nly one that you can be.
G et your chart and you will see.
Y our dreams or hopes were meant to be.

Ross Gardiner (12)
Blackwood Comprehensive School

ZODIAC

Deep, dark, mysterious is what it appears to be,
Bright, glistening, magical stars are part of what we see.

Nine planets are part of our distant solar system,
Astronauts on missions, for noises they listen.

Are there other lives up there all of us wonder?
Aliens, humans, insects, our brains are in a blunder.

A fireball, huger than our Earth shines like heaven,
To look at it for hours is not so clever.

Shooting stars race across the sky,
Faster than a cheetah looking for its prey.

I watch them so softly and silently as I can,
But not in the day.

Sarah Bettell-Higgins (14)
Blackwood Comprehensive School

UNTITLED

In the sky there are millions of stars,
Planets too, Jupiter, Venus, Neptune and Mars.
Sometimes I wonder why
We don't see other planets passing us by?
I mean, are there such things as UFOs?
No one knows.
Stars and planets really puzzle me
I really don't understand astrology.

Sinéad Brennan (13)
Blackwood Comprehensive School

SCORPIO

My star sign is Scorpio,
It crawls around the floor.
It looks really horrible from a book,
But I don't think in real life it would be as bad.

I hate creepy-crawly things,
Especially spiders or snakes.
If I see anything creepy beside me I will faint,
So I would hate my star sign.

Laura Yip (12)
Blackwood Comprehensive School

MY STAR SIGN

P   isces
I   s a star sign
S   agittarius is another, so is
C   ancer
E   veryone has got a
S   tar sign, so what is yours?

Sara Wright (11)
Blackwood Comprehensive School

HAMSTERS

Hamsters are very, very funny,
Their fur is thick, soft and fluffy.
They have big teeth which they keep neat.
They run everywhere using their tiny feet.
I like hamsters, do you?

Philip Thomas (12)
Blackwood Comprehensive School

STAR SIGN

All star signs stand for something.
They describe what type of person you are.
The signs are based on how the moon looks
And not what is said in some star sign books.

They range from Aries to Pisces, which amounts to twelve in all.
Each has their own meaning, even though some are small.
There are people who claim to know how the moon works,
But some of these are just berks.

One famous person is Mystic Meg
She works on TV to forecast the Lottery.
She tells which star sign will win the loot,
But sometimes I think she should get the boot.

I don't think she gets it right all the time.
Maybe she should pick more than one sign.
I was born on 20th June,
A Gemini sign which is all mine.

Daniel Russell (11)
Blackwood Comprehensive School

ZODIAC!

There are twelve signs of the zodiac,
A different sign for a different track,
Where astrologers read your star,
This is what we are told from the planets afar.

Mine is Pisces, the sign of the fish.
Jon Bon Jovi is Pisces to my favourite dish,
Printed in the paper day after day,
Predicting your future or so they say.

It's hard to believe the stars are right,
But if mine came true then I just might,
So I'll just keep ready day after day,
Just to check what they have to say.

Tanya Mellens (13)
Blackwood Comprehensive School

SCORPIOS

S   corpions, they say, are a very good breed,
C   onscientious and caring, without any greed.
O   ne for a friend, then you've a good friend for life.
R   eliable and trustworthy, they won't cause you strife.
P   lacid in nature, unless they're truly provoked,
I   nspirational, quick-witted and loves a good joke.
O   ne word of advice though, if you don't mind,
S   incerity and honesty will see you repaid in kind.

Jason Williams (13)
Blackwood Comprehensive School

SCHOOL

They say school is the best time of your life
Sometimes I find it's nothing but strife
English and biology I think are fine
But maths and science are a bit of a bind
When I grow up and become someone's wife
I'll agree what they say
School was the best time of my life.

Jodie Lee Shankland (12)
Blackwood Comprehensive School

THE SIGNS OF THE ZODIAC

Virgo, the virgin,
The lady of men's dreams.
Pisces, the fish,
Swimming through the oceans.
Sagittarius, the archer,
Whose everlasting arrows shoot through the sky.
Gemini, the twins,
The troublesome pair.
Aquarius, the water carrier,
The provider of life.
Capricorn, the goat,
He guides us through the problems.
Leo, the lion,
His huge roar keeps us safe.
Libra, the scales,
Keeping the balance of time.
Scorpio, the scorpion,
With a sting in its tail.
Taurus, the bull,
Charging all our enemies.
Cancer, the crab,
With a sideways walk and snappy pincers.
Aries, the ram,
He provides our food and clothes for all our needs.

Hannah Spillett (11)
Blackwood Comprehensive School

YOUR STARS

Taurus and Pisces and Aquarius,
Gemini, Cancer and Leo.
Libra and Aries and Sagittarius,
Scorpio, Capricorn and Virgo.

There're so many animals to see where you are.
You can call it your horoscope or your star.
There're all different shapes and sizes too.
Don't act your age, act the size of your shoe!

Kerys Williams (12)
Blackwood Comprehensive School

ZODIAC

Shooting stars in the sky,
Flying high all night long,
Up there really high,
Leo, the lion lies
Along by another star Gemini.
No one knows how high they fly,
Except the stars in the sky,
Shining bright all night,
Until the sun rises.

Matthew Rees (13)
Blackwood Comprehensive School

THE ZODIAC

Z odiac across the dark, black sky
O ver us they look, those twinkling stars
D rawn as different pictures, Virgo is one
I f you don't know what I'm on about
A nd you want your fortune told, listen up
C os it's the zodiac!

Vicki Pugh (12)
Blackwood Comprehensive School

ZODIAC

There was a great man from Mars,
He lived way up in the stars,
He drives round in cars,
But he still stays well hidden, up in Mars.

There is a man in Heaven,
Who used to live in Devon.
He moved from Devon to Heaven
After being caught breaking into Cefn.

There is a shop in the sky,
It sold me my favourite tie
It also sells nice pies.
All from my favourite shop in the sky.

My favourite time is night,
To see what's going on
You need very good sight.
I love to look outside, even when
There is no light.

Rhodri Isaacs (12)
Blackwood Comprehensive School

MY ZODIAC POEM

Pisces the fish, cool as ice
Aries the ram was a sacrifice
Taurus the bull fought but who wins
Next comes Gemini, the heavenly twins.

Cancer the crab, a scare to men
Here's Leo the lion in his den.
Virgo for the virgin Mary
Libra the scales was really scary.

Scorpio the scorpion wanted to fight
Sagittarius the arch used all his might.
Capricorn the goat was no warrior,
Aquarius was the water carrier.

Emma Perry (12)
Blackwood Comprehensive School

ZODIAC

Way up high in outer space,
The zodiac came into place.
They're shooting stars in the night sky,
The astronomers never lie.

There're twelve star signs in the zodiac,
With information they never lack.
Pisces, Taurus and Aquarius
Altogether they are very mysterious.

The ones at which I like to glance
Are the ones that tell me about romance.

Amy Lee King (13)
Blackwood Comprehensive School

ZODIAC

Taurus, the big strong bull
Cancer the bright red crab
Leo the big angry lion
Aries the nasty ram
Scorpio the poisonous scorpion
Pisces the fast and sleek fish
Virgo the shy virgin.

Natalie Marie Lucas (12)
Blackwood Comprehensive School

THE PARK

The smell of the green, green grass,
The squeaking of the swings,
The flowery smell as you go past,
And the sound of a bird's flapping wings.

Butterflies on the trees,
The sound of children's laughter,
The lovely summer breeze,
And the playful dogs you'll run after.

In the pond some lazy fish,
The people having fun,
On the picnic table, some fruit in a dish,
But warm from the blazing hot sun.

Sara Edwards (11)
Blackwood Comprehensive School

THE STAR SIGNS

Of the twelve stars in the sky
One of them belongs to I,
The one that does is called Aquarius,
Not Aries or Sagittarius.

Aquarius is the water carrier,
Swimming away from the warrior.
The water carrier swims away
Allowing the warrior to stay.

Leo the lion can be brave
Often risks his life to save.
Pisces is the fishy one
When Taurus comes we all must run.

Aimee Meredith (12)
Blackwood Comprehensive School

ZODIAC

There are twelve signs of the zodiac and each one has a name.

An Arian is a leader who is energetic and takes risks,
Intolerant, jealous, selfish and impulsive.

A Taurean is artistic, attentive, very loving and calm.
Is boring, insensitive, stubborn and has little to say.

Geminians are versatile, youthful, inquisitive and inventive.
Get bored quickly, are nervous and have a duel personality.

A Cancerian is tenacious, kind and compassionate.
Possessive, moody, crabby and too easily hurt.

A Leonian is honest, loyal, generous and kind,
Arrogant, smug, stubborn and cold-hearted.

Virgoans are organised, sympathetic, witty and dedicated.
Untidy, cranky, nervous and prudish.

Librans are refined, artistic, charming and sincere.
Fearful, flirtatious, narcissistic and over-coming.

Scorpians are magnetic, dynamic, intense and sensual.
Ruthless, dangerous, sadistic and vindictive.

Sagittarians are frank, optimistic, inspiring
happy-go-lucky, hot-headed, argumentative,
uncommitted and indulgent.

Capricornians are cautious, conventional and concerned.
Egotistical, fatalistic, anxious and unforgiving.

Aquarians are inventive, communicate, thoughtful and scientific.
Tactless, rude, self-interested and perverse.

Piscians are shy, helpful, romantic and mystical.
Temperamental, dependent, depressive and gullible.

Siän Louise Fuller (13)
Blackwood Comprehensive School

ZODIAC

On a cold and frosty night, when the stars shine so bright,
The whole world they seem to fight.
When a shooting star falls to earth, I make a wish with some mirth.

The whole constellation makes an awesome sight,
The stars are so many light years away, yet seem so near at night.

There are millions of stars, yet one shone bright many years ago.
It's said this star of Bethlehem heralded the birth of Jesus in a
                                                    manger stall.

Capricorn, Aquarius, Aries and Pisces are a few to name
There are so many, some with flame.

The birth and death of a star takes millions of years,
Some we see but others never I fear.

Kayleigh Bidgway (12)
Blackwood Comprehensive School

WHAT'S MY FATE

Check the newspaper,
What does it say?
Will I have a good day?

Win the lottery?
Find some nice pottery?
Will the stars align?
Lucky for my sign.

Zodiac, zodiac
Who will it be?
Is there someone out there for me?
Love, luck, fortune!

Ben Rowberry (12)
Blackwood Comprehensive School

WAY ABOVE THE EARTH

The mysterious night,
That holds no light,
Other than the moon and the stars:

Stores other wonders,
And while the world slumbers,
They prowl the midnight sky.

Shooting stars and constellations,
Wonders of our God's creation,
Shape our world around:

Uranus, Pluto, Saturn and Mars,
Can all leave our lives with scars,
But we can't question why?

Carly Jade Watkins (13)
Blackwood Comprehensive School

JOURNEY THROUGH THE STARS

The sun, the moon, the planets
and stars.
Uranus, Pluto, Neptune and Mars.
Meteorites, asteroids and shooting stars.
Silvers, gold and reddy Mars.
Too close to the sun and you will melt.
Comets shoot across Orion's Belt.
Through Milky Way and galaxy bars,
This is your journey through the stars.

Rhian Gamlin (13)
Blackwood Comprehensive School

THE BEST SKY THAT I EVER DID SEE

A fortune teller once said to me,
The best sky I ever would see,
Was in a place called Italy.

The clear sky, dark in the night,
Not a sound or cloud in sight.
Twinkling like a diamond ring,
Like a sparkling crystal in the sky.

I wish I could grow wings and learn to fly,
I look up and what can I see?
A shooting star passing me.
I make a wish
Now what can that be?
That I could be in Italy.

Ieuan Wall (11)
Blackwood Comprehensive School

THE ZODIAC

All the stars flying around,
Making space dark and bound.

As we look in the sky,
We can see Gemini.

As the twins look right back,
We can see the zodiac.

All the stars up above,
They will tell us wealth and love.

As the stars tell us our lives,
Other people think they're lies.

Ross Lewis Forbes (13)
Blackwood Comprehensive School

CANCER

One star sign is Cancer,
You are guaranteed to be a dancer.
One of your colours is grey,
And Monday is your best day.

Your animal is a crab
And all your foods are fab.
Pearl is your gemstone,
You're in your next time zone.

Your personality is the best,
It's better than all the rest.
We are so very kind,
We have the best mind.

Next is your love,
They call you the dove.
You love your loved ones
And maybe you'll become a nun.

Katie Reynolds (12)
Blackwood Comprehensive School

THE STARS

Zodiac is the stars
One group of them is ours.
Aquarius, Cancer, Capricorn, Scorpio,
Pisces, Taurus, Gemini and Leo.

Stargazers gaze at the stars at night
Under the bright moonlight.
While I sleep in bed
And think about stars in my head.

Claire Gwilt (13)
Blackwood Comprehensive School

MY ZODIAC

My zodiac,
What is that?
What does it mean
That I read in the mag?

It tells me to be money careful,
Only my pocket is empty not full.
Love is good for me at this time,
But girls drive me up the wall.

Now it says I should change my job,
I don't work, I live as a slob.
Exercise would be a good idea,
What's it saying, I'm a blob?

These zodiac signs
Don't read like mine.
I'll live how I like,
My life is just fine.

Mark Evans (12)
Blackwood Comprehensive School

THE ZODIAC POEM

Some people read their star signs,
Some people don't.
There are all kinds of signs,
Twelve in all.
Sometimes you can see your star signs
In the night.
Astrologers study star signs
Every day and night.

Michael John Carey (11)
Blackwood Comprehensive School

PAUL?

Beyond the clouds, beyond the sky
I sense something else, an alien boy.
Will he be fat? Will he be thin?
Will he smell like a wheelie bin?

Will he be hairy? Will he be scary?
Will he have wings and look like a fairy?
Will he be tall? Will he be small?
I wonder if his name is Paul?

I wonder what all my friends would say
If my intergalactic friend was gay?
How will he get here? How will we know?
Will he fly down in his UFO?
Where is he hiding? Where does he stay?
I'm sure we'll find out some day?

Aaron Williams (13)
Blackwood Comprehensive School

ZODIAC

I looked up at the dazzling sky and saw the stars shape into my star
sign Cancer.
Some days I wish I knew the story behind our star signs and others,
well not as much.
Every night I look up at the stars and see what different star sign
twinkles tonight.
The small twinkling stars look lovely up against the black velvet night
sky from a distance.
From this day forward everyone gathers together on the hill and stares
at the night sky.

Siân Haynes (11)
Blackwood Comprehensive School

ZODIAC POEM

Heaven:

There was a boy
who lived in Devon
he went to Heaven
when he was eleven.

Stars:

There was a man who lived in the stars,
where there were lots of bars
he could see Venus and Mars
sitting right under the stars.

Sky

There was a man who visited the sky,
there he bought an enormous pie,
amongst the hours that went by
the man just sat there in the dark night sky.

Daniel Jefferies (12)
Blackwood Comprehensive School

ZODIAC

Z ena predicts my horoscope
O ften gets it wrong
D oesn't really matter
I always go along
A ddicted to reading my stars
C ould be influenced by Venus or Mars.

Naomi Jenkins (13)
Blackwood Comprehensive School

THE WORLD

A beautiful sky, the deep blue sea
How calm and beautiful for all to see.
With singing birds and flowers in spring
What better things in life to bring.

The grass is green, the daisies are white,
Different colours on flowers makes everything bright.
The dawn, the dusk, the twilight too
There's more things in life to bring to you.

The world is like a garden
The world is like the sea,
Put them both together
It will make a world for you and me.

Rachael Davies (12)
Blackwood Comprehensive School

ZODIAC!

Who made up astrology?
The zodiac?
The stars we see?

The tiger, the rooster,
The dragon, the horse.
The monkey, the rat.
Oh, and the dog of course.

Space is so far away.
It is different to our land in many ways.
Stars, comets, planets galore.
So many things to love and adore.

Rebecca Gough (13)
Blackwood Comprehensive School

ZODIAC POEM

There are nine planets in our universe,
Examples of these are Mars, Venus and Earth
Numerous planets have moons and a sun
The zodiac has existed since time begun.

A few of these star signs are Scorpio,
Gemini and Aquarius.
Also there are Aries, Taurus, Virgo and Sagittarius.
They are divided into Water, Air, Earth and Fire,
Horoscopes hope to bring you good fortune and desire.

The seventh sign of the zodiac is Libra, the scales.
Librans excel themselves in lots of different ways.
September is my birth month, Libra is my sign.
I read about the day ahead and hope
Good luck will be mine!

Helen Eynon (13)
Blackwood Comprehensive School

ZODIAC

As I gaze up at the sky at night,
the stars are twinkling and shining bright.
The clusters of stars make different forms,
the fish, the bull, I can see his horns.
Aries, Cancer, Leo, Aquarius,
Virgo, Libra, Scorpio, Sagittarius.
They're all up there twinkling bright,
in the cold, black sky at night.

Kyle Pockett (12)
Blackwood Comprehensive School

ZODIAC

Z   ooming stars cross the sky
O   dd shapes passing by
D   azzling stars twinkle high
I   ncredible lights glowing
A   quarius, Leo - zodiac signs
C   apricorn and Scorpio too.

Ian Kibble (12)
Blackwood Comprehensive School

A TOUCH OF AUTUMN

The crisp autumn leaves
drizzled and flowed
in the early morning breeze

As the big chunky conkers
toppled from the trees

The grass rushed green
and the dew splashed

As children dashed,
back and forth in the
farmer's fields

Muffled leaves crunch and crackle
like a gumwood fire and
rustle like fidgety children

The sun is breezy
yet warm and humid
another touch of autumn
has ended.

Myscha-Dene Bates (12)
King Henry VIII School

THE LIFE OF ANIMALS

I'm an animal
A lion
I think what I like
And
I do what I like
I know how I'm treated
Good or bad.

I look at other animals
I try to get into their head
Find out what they're thinking

I see how they've been treated
The sad thing is I see how
They've been treated,
But I can't do anything

I've not been treated as badly
Animals like my friends and I
Should not be treated this bad

No animal should be treated badly.

We are what we are, and that's life!

Kirsty R House (13)
King Henry VIII School

THIS IS A CHOCOLATE BAR

This is the chocolate bar that's very yummy
It is brown, sweet and nice in my tummy.
It's very nice, tasty too
But it's mine, and not for you!

Emily Thomas (12)
King Henry VIII School

A BEER COMPETITION

You win or you lose
But still gulp the booze,
Friends just laugh and joke
You should have resorted to fizzy Coke.

The final has now come about
All the drunks start to shout,
The winner's arm is casually raised
By the drunken chaps he is praised.

The medallion placed around his neck
He is drunk and his mind's a wreck.
He is a victor in his eyes
The others couldn't win with a million.

Now it's time to celebrate
He's so drunk he can't walk straight,
The beer is on the house to him
He gulps 'em down right from the rim.

He is dreading getting back
His wife will give him lots of slack,
He clambers off the mini-bus
His wife on the doorstep, ready for a fuss.

Now he knows it was a bad idea
Drinking all that Heineken beer,
Sorry! Was all he could say
You should have seen him the very next day!

James Bevan (12)
King Henry VIII School

MY BROTHER

The wind howled and hissed
I stood amongst the dead
I looked at the gravestone
       Matthew Peter Turnbull.

He was gone
And I was left alone.

An ice-cold tear
Trickled down my face
Running my make-up
       All down my cheek.

He was gone
And I was left alone.

For he has burned a hole in my heart,
But he will stay with me
In my life
And in my soul.

He was gone
And I was left alone

Bryony Turnbull (13)
King Henry VIII School

NAN!

I looked up at the stars,
The brightest one shone like the moon,
A tear ran down my cheek
Left and then right.

'Nan! Why did it happen to you?
Forever I thought you would live,
Great balls of fire,
Couldn't keep me away from you.

I love you Nan
And I always will.
With all the bad things that happen in life,
I will always look to talk to you.'

Eloise Heffernan (12)
King Henry VIII School

AUNTY NANCY

When I first met you I was young,
You offered me over, oh, what fun.

When I came over I made lots of noise,
Playing with the dinosaur toys.

When I came over I watched you knit,
You were the one who got me doing it.

When I came over we watched 15 to 1
On my way home I had to run.

When I came over it was fun,
You made my dinners, they filled my tum.

When I came over, Countdown was great
We watched for ages, till it was late.

But now's the time to say 'Goodbye!'
Now you're gone we cry and cry.

This poem is dedicated to a friend
Who was like a Nan to me, whom I loved very much.

Aunty Nancy
RIP

Rebecca Williams (12)
King Henry VIII School

ROBIN HUNTING

I know you may think that I have a funny name
But I have a hunting job.
My name is Robin Hood, some may say
But this is not true of course.

'Robin, Robin!' A girl said to me
'I think you're great . . . super.
I'd love to be your princess
So would you be my prince?'

To be a married man
I don't know if I can,
For some women love me more
Than this woman does, for sure.

Claire Pugh (12)
King Henry VIII School

LIFE OF A DOG

I'm locked up in a shed every day and night,
I can't see a thing as there is no light,
Nothing to eat for days and days
I want to escape, I try many ways.
My bark of misery is never heard.
Oh how I wish I was a bird,
Flying high above the trees
Freedom, power, can do as I please.
My brown matted fur that's full of dirt,
No one to brush me, so I can convert,
So I can be a well kept tidy dog,
Instead of my life being like a bleak fog.

Naomi Cole (13)
King Henry VIII School

STARS THAT SPELL OUT FATE

Combined stars
Spell out fate
The atmosphere surrounding
I sit and wait:

Libra stands out in the shape of the scales,
According to Centaurs, it never fails.

Aquarius is there as a water carrier,
If this is your fate, you'll see no barriers.

Taurus twists into the shape of a bull,
If this is your sign, you see the glass as half full.

There is no point telling you the other few
Because these are star signs, they're not true!

Kate Mills (12)
King Henry VIII School

LION

I wasn't always here
Performing for people
I was in my real home
Wild and free
With my own kind of company
Taken from there when I was a cub
Every day is now the same
Light is the beginning
Repeating the same things
I'm the only lion here
Alone.

Charlotte Rees (13)
King Henry VIII School

UNTITLED

Flying over a sandy desert,
Loud noises such as gunfire and explosions up ahead.
That burning smell in the air,
Soldiers fighting for their loved ones
And their countries.

Bombs dropping from the sky,
It's times like these, I'm glad to fly.
People running below me,
But there is nowhere to run to or hide.
Death below me
They know that their time may come.

I came towards a city
The people must been terrified.
All they can see is pain
And blood running down the drain.
They see the rubble on the floor,
The city, destroyed for ever more.

Kane Bray (13)
King Henry VIII School

CAGED UP!

I've lived all my life in this strong metal cage,
Never been free to let out my rage.
I'm fed through the bars each day and night,
People are scared, they fear I may bite.
Crowds gather round to point and stare,
They don't seem to think my life is unfair.
Some of the animals caged up like me
Got their wish and have been set free.

Pippa Jones (13)
King Henry VIII School

THE SEASONS

Spring is here, it's warm and wet,
Children out playing football,
The daffodils show off their yellow colours
Whilst birds hum their tunes in the sky.

Next comes summer. It's so hot.
People sunbathing on their deckchairs.
Children buying loads of ice creams
Then into the sea for a refreshing swim.

Leaves are falling from the trees,
Everyone knows autumn is here.
It's getting colder and trees are bare,
Hallowe'en scares even the bravest of people.

Winter is here, it's very cold
Santa is ready to deliver his presents.
Children hang their stockings at the end of their beds,
Waiting to be filled with wonderful presents.

Tom Carrett (12)
King Henry VIII School

THE VOID

Screaming silently through the void of space,
Stars and galaxies, galaxies of stars,
Rocket past the window out here, wherever here is.
A ghostly light filters in to mix with the rest,
Life drifts past at light speed, just a handful.
Surely not enough to colonise a universe?
Is that where we are, a universe or one of many?
Who knows? We're closest to wherever here is!
In the void of space, screaming silently by.

Leo Jofeh (13)
King Henry VIII School

IN VERONA

In Verona a tragedy takes place
Two households who are such bitter enemies,
Fighting and quarrelling when face to face,
Are the Montague and Capulet families.
Rosaline is Romeo's love in life,
Is Paris the right man for Juliet?
Rosaline will not be Romeo's wife
Juliet Capulet, he has not yet met.
The Capulet and Montague servants fight,
Only the Capulets to attend the feast.
With a warning at the feast, it's all right
As Romeo arrives, that little beast.
The first time Romeo sees Juliet -
This is the girl he will never forget.

Stephanie Macpherson (13)
King Henry VIII School

WRITING A LETTER

Writing a letter is great fun
Before you know it, you are done,
Letters go all around the world
Some to boys, some to girls.
Different fonts are sometimes used,
And sometimes the postman lose
Your favourite piece of news.
Some are addressed Mr, Ms or Mrs
And some say 'Best Wishes'
And most have lots of kisses.

Katie Moss (12)
King Henry VIII School

My Feelings

I can be good and
I can be bad

I can be happy and
I can be sad

I can be sweet and
I can be sour

I can be quiet and
I can scream for an hour

I can be kind and
I can be helpful

I can be honest and
I can be doubtful

I can be good and
I can be bad

I can be happy and
I can be sad.

Kirsty Williams (12)
King Henry VIII School

Elephant's Tusks

We live in India in the heat
Hoping hunters we don't meet
All they want is the tusks from me
Which leaves the effected in agony
Every day we pray and pray
It wouldn't be us, the very next day

David Bowen (13)
King Henry VIII School

MUNDANE MONDAY

I wake up and stare at my alarm clock
It hisses and groans with a fierce tick-tock
It's 7 o'clock! I want to sleep!
And dream and count fluffy, white sheep
But it's Monday.

I brush my teeth and comb my hair,
And give my mother a fierce glare.
She refused to let me stay off school.
So now I must face the swimming pool
Because it's Monday.

I walk grumpily up to the bus
And I kick up a great, big fuss.
The bus is there, ready to go!
But I am not, cos I'm so slow.
Because it's Monday.

It's now first lesson. Triumph! Glee!
I think really sarcastically.
He's collecting homework. I feel dead
Because it's at home upon my bed.
What a Monday!

Lunchtime now, I feel great!
Until I see what's on my plate.
Bangers and mash, spotted dick
I run to the bathroom, I'm going to be sick!
Because it's Monday.

I go home, I think *yeah!*
Then I realise tomorrow is another day.
Another place, another Hell.
And the dreaded ring of that school bell.
And I hate it! *Every day!*

Louise Brown (13)
King Henry VIII School

MY WAR POEM

The sirens rip open the dark sky
I could hear it in my hut
Bang, bang! Guns and bombs.
The soldiers were quick to fight.
Some were dead
Some were alive
Some had very bad cuts.
I felt very scared
Aeroplanes flew over
And ships were coming across the sea.
Life had never been so bad
I was stuck in the middle.
I didn't know what to do.
Out go the soldiers
Ready to kill.
There are their guns
All types.
I can hear bangs and crashes.
People falling to the ground.
At last they said the
War was over!
We had joy at last.

Ben Mian (13)
King Henry VIII School

HAVE YOU EVER?

Come to my house, it's not that far,
You can travel there on a shooting star.
Have you ever had a taste of the moon?
The cheese is good, you can have some soon.
Have you ever played football with an alien or two?
You don't need a football, any bright star will do.
Have you ever seen the stars
Whilst having a picnic on Jupiter or Mars?
Have you ever been to an alien school?
The creatures that go there are really cool.
So hurry up, we will be there soon,
My little space house on the moon.

Kelly Rubbery (13)
King Henry VIII School

SPACE

The stars and planets all whizzing past,
coming towards me in such a blast.
Planets round, astronauts floating, sparkling stars
and rockets passing.
I see the stars in a light,
shining so bright, bright, bright.
The moon lighting up the sky so everyone
can see when they go by.
Venus, Mercury, Pluto and Mars,
all together just go past.
Flying saucers go round and round
All circling, nowhere to be found.

Annmarie Kelly (14)
King Henry VIII School

THE LIFE OF THE STARS

The glittering diamonds shining at night,
The patterns of planets, the frosty moonlight.
Out come the mystical creatures unknown,
Into our twinkling eyes they are shown.

Taurus, Cancer, Aries and Leo
Gemini, Virgo and Scorpio,
Capricorn, Sagittarius,
Libra, Pisces and Aquarius.

The magical spirits, angelic guide
Will lead us through our full lives wide,
As glittering stars, they fill us with care,
And return to their wonderful homes, up there.

So when you dream in your bed at night,
Look at the sky, a fabulous sight,
And sleep with a star shining in your mind,
And leave all your worries and troubles behind.

Natalie Marshall (13)
King Henry VIII School

STAR SIGNS

A lways ready to come and get you
Q uietly creeping right down to the ground
U ranus is above me, as I proudly bound
A waiting new arrivals, I slowly wound
R ound, round, and round again
I like to see you up above
U nder me as well you see
S omebody on Earth will be just like me.

Hannah James (13)
King Henry VIII School

AT THE BORDER

They call for my ineffectual help,
I register into something I know nothing about.
Suddenly I am in the abysmal death of the once countryside.
I inhale the virus through the harmonic beats of my lungs.
I raise my head over the uneven line of the trench edge,
Short flashes of light destroy the darkness.
The sound of war breaks into the minds of soldiers,
Disoriented and confused, they lie helplessly in the mud.
I trudge through the mangled road hill,
Lying on my living room floor.
As I step into the raging torrent of shells and bullets
The fiery flame is raised to my cigar.
I crawl further into the blood-soaked grass,
A bullet is shot into my wound
I was registered . . . I was.

Vien Taeed (13)
King Henry VIII School

STARS IN THE NIGHT SKY

Twinkle, twinkle gleaming star,
Shining in the bright high sky.
There I was in the fresh green grass,
making the patterns of the
shining stars.
There are millions of planets
in the sky
now it's time to say goodbye
as I make my way
across the sky.

Stacey Warner (13)
King Henry VIII School

ROMEO AND JULIET

Two lovers from families who both hate,
Juliet and Romeo are their names,
The families' quarrels end in their fate,
The end of their lives burns out hatred's flame.
It began with the Capulet's feast,
Where no Montague wanted to be found.
But Romeo's love had now ceased
And he was found on the Capulet's grounds.
Romeo had never seen such beauty
As Juliet, until this night
Tybalt saw him and did his duty,
But was told by Capulet not to fight,
The two enemies met and fell in love,
But spent their lives in the world up above.

Megan Bransom (13)
King Henry VIII School

HOROSCOPES

I look at my horoscope today
What luck will come my way?
Love, or money, will come soon?
No! 'Venus enters Neptune!'
What does that mean? I think.
I look at the weird letters in ink,
I see what it says for Tuesday.
Whoo! *'You'll express yourself brilliantly today!'*

Oh good, I hope it comes true,
But horoscopes never do!

Kate Busby (13)
King Henry VIII School

CRIMINAL COLLEGE!

Arriving at twenty past eight
Never-ending slavery
From morning to end
Bells ring for twenty minute of freedom
Then back to the dark, dingy depths of the school
Without the privilege of sitting next to a friend
Hours of work
Fingers wearing to the bone
Lines upon lines of chalky punishment
Prison keepers pushing to drain your fingers of blood
Keeping you in after the freedom bell has rung
Left-over food from yesterday is that which
We are expected to eat.
Alas, it is over, but still they give us
Brain bending work to stop us from
Having fun!

Toby Meredith (13)
King Henry VIII School

THE ZODIAC

Looking up into the sparkling sky
As my mum sings a lullaby.
The Great Bear and the Little Bear too
Looking down from far above you.
Leo the Lion, a giant, big thing,
In the jungle he's a king.
The Crab in the sky, that's Cancer,
Strutting his stuff, like a professional dancer.
Writing this poem, I've had a great time,
I hope you've enjoyed my stargazing rhyme.

Rachel Knight (13)
King Henry VIII School

THE SKY

In the sky there are stars
In the sky there is Mars
In the sky there is a moon
In the sky there is a sun
It is round and looks like a bun -
The sky is lovely and clear
When you look up it's near
All the planets are all colourful
Rockets are fast
You never see men go past
All the planets are called Saturn, Jupiter,
Venus, Mars, Pluto and Mercury.
In the sky, the clouds are big
At night the moon is out
It's big and white
It's a lovely sight
The planets and the stars go whizzing past
They go really fast
The sky is lovely
I love the sky.

Kirsty Yemm (13)
King Henry VIII School

BONFIRE NIGHT

Lights, lights everywhere,
In the sky and on the ground,
Green, blue, yellow, orange, pink and red
Bonfires that warm you up,
Or fireworks that light up the sky,
The sparklers are fun to use.
Oh I just can't wait until Bonfire Night.

Gareth James (11)
King Henry VIII School

NOVEMBER THE 5TH

Boom, boom, sparkle, sparkle,
Hear them crash in the night sky,
See the colourful lights brighten up the dark, dark sky.

There are Catherine wheels that make a whizzing sound
And bangers that go *bang, bang,*
Look up in the sky and you can see bright, shiny, sparkly colours,
With your noses you can smell burning logs,
See the burning fire, big and red.

Little children dress up warm
With their little mittens, hat and scarf on,
Making patterns with sparklers.

Another November the 5th has come and gone
And now winter is on its way.

Giselle Quarrington (11)
King Henry VIII School

THE BROOK

It starts like this,
Trickles gently down the mountain top
Then it widens, it quickens, it is rockier
It flows like rapids over rocks,
Then it crashes down the waterfall.
It flows gently again
Past the little cottages
Into the river,
The dirty, murky river,
Again and again and again!

Gareth Roberts (12)
King Henry VIII School

THE ZODIAC

The Plough is a saucepan
Bubbling up with soup,
Tomato, veg or chicken.
Free range or from the coop.
Orion is a lonely man,
His belt glitters all night,
If only he could find a girl
Then he'd shine really bright!
The seven sisters, those cheeky girls,
Go out every night with golden curls,
They fight and quarrel, hit and kick,
Get out! Get out! You have to be quick!
You'll find yourself very pleased.
I hope you'll like this, don't send it back,
My poem about the zodiac.

Rhiannon Wells (11)
King Henry VIII School

OH WHAT A DAY

Wales V Ireland, what a day,
Wales lost, but it's OK,
No one played a very good game,
But Ireland won all the same,
Wales were rubbish they didn't play well,
Our passing was appalling, our handling as well.
Ireland had won right from the start,
You should have seen the poor Welshmen
It broke their hearts,
All I can say to the Irish is good luck,
Hope you can beat England
And put them in the muck.

Tom Vaughan (12)
King Henry VIII School

A LITTLE POEM

Some poems are dead boring,
so I thought I might arrange
a short but funny, senseless poem,
just to make a change.

I'll start off with Lucy,
and her little duck,
it came into the house one day
and covered it with muck.

The duck was in deep trouble,
Lucy was in a state,
and in the end the poor, old duck,
ended up on the plate.

I hope this poem made you laugh,
because it certainly did me,
but now I'd really like some more duck,
so it's off to the kitchen with me!

Patrick O'Malley (11)
King Henry VIII School

STARS

I like space and all the stars,
The Milky Way and scrummy Mars
All the stars are big and bright,
Shining in the sky at night.

Pluto is so very cold
Jupiter is big and bold,
Venus a romantic place
Neptune so far out in space.

Stars shine brightly every night,
They are pretty full of light,
The sun, biggest star of all,
Makes the rest ever so small.

Katie Edmondson (14)
King Henry VIII School

ELEMENTS

Fire

Hear the crackling flames of the fire
The reds and the oranges dancing.
See the smoke rise higher and higher
Little sparks leaping and prancing.

Earth

Look at the Earth, at all the bright colours
Look at the rocks and the trees,
Look at the sky, the road even duller.
Look around, what can you see?

Water

Hear the trickling droplets of dew,
The waves of the sea crashing.
Feel the rain flood down on you,
The water in the stream splashing.

Air

Feel the wisps of the wind in the air,
The voice of the wind howling.
Taste the coldness of the night everywhere
The whispers of the wind prowling.

Kate Hanbury (12)
King Henry VIII School

CANCER IS MY STAR SIGN

Cancer is my star sign,
Charlotte is my name,
Cancer is luxurious,
Cancer is insane.

It mostly predicts good luck,
It sometimes predicts bad,
I wish upon my lucky star,
That it never gives me bad.

Cancer tells a story,
The story of my life,
My life is very lovely,
And I hope it stays like that.

Cancer is my star sign,
Charlotte is my name,
Cancer is luxurious,
Cancer is insane.

Charlotte Morris (11)
King Henry VIII School

SHEEP

They were sent down to study our race
Millions of years ago,
They originally hated us,
Our greatest foe!

They roamed our land, searching for
Our Achilles heel,
They couldn't find it and soon became
Our next meal!

Soon they will fight back
Our land they will keep,
Because they are powerful
They are . . . *sheep!*

Kelan Handley (12)
King Henry VIII School

STARS, STARS, STARS

Leo, Leo the lion
I'm made of iron,
I know people think stars are a myth
And my birthday is in August, it's August 5th.
I believe in the stars,
Some people think I'm from Mars.

Stars for March, April and May,
Some say you may lose pay.
Stars for July, August and September,
What do you need to remember?

Star signs are great,
I read them with my mate,
Stars come out at night,
I read them in daylight.

The zodiac is in the sky,
Do the star signs lie?
Are they made up?
They say I will get a pup.
I believe in my star signs,
This is the end of my lines.

Michaela Williams (13)
King Henry VIII School

MY PERFECT DAY

My perfect day that I dream of, I know will never be made.
This is a compound of all my favourite things
Which I love, like and delight in.
My perfect day would be a Saturday
I would spend it with my grampy
In the white garden,
The crisp, clean snow around us, crunching under feet.
Snowmen in the corner, snowballs flying past.
This is one of my favourite days.
I open the kitchen door
The gorgeous smell of roast dinner invites me in,
Now I know it's time for tea.
I look around at the table, piled high with food
To please me.
Now I'm nearly full, just a little more space
For my perfect dessert . . .
A chocolate sundae and a chocolate milkshake.
Cosy, warm and very well fed,
I'm feeling really sleepy
Now I know it's time for bed.
I climb the stairs, thinking of my day.
Waiting to dream my perfect dream of another day.

Natasha Matthews (13)
King Henry VIII School

TAURUS, TAURUS

Taurus, Taurus, do you think he saw us?
If we wore red
He will ram us in the head
We'll end up dead
We'd rather go to bed!

Geraint Hatherall (11)
King Henry VIII School

THE SOLDIER

Inching my way on enemy grounds
My corporal whispered 'Hey!
Shoot that man upon that mound
Of rubble. Is that okay?'

First I took out my gun
And aimed it at his head.
Then I pulled back my rifle trigger
Bang! He dropped down dead.

An enemy soldier heard the shot
And shouted to his army.
So I stood up and ran the other way
For I was brave, not barmy.

After a few minutes of running,
I came to a fresh water stream.
So I filled up my water bottle
But behind me I heard a scream.

I turned around quite quickly
And saw my team retreat.
So I took out my SA80
And shot that German fleet.

I got a medal for bravery
It was the second best day of my life,
The first was when the war was over
And I went home to my loving wife.

Rhys Davies (12)
King Henry VIII School

SHOOTING STARS

Gazing at the sky,
Stars so far away,
They twinkle in the night,
But vanish in the day.

Almost in a second,
There is a blast of light,
Like a bullet from a gun,
But only in the night.

A sparkling, shining star,
Shooting far across the sky,
Crossing over hungry oceans,
Will it ever die?

As fast as a running cheetah,
It shines like the sun,
Circling the world,
It's having such fun.

Sparkling, spinning star,
Makes not a single sound,
No buzz, no swoosh, no murmur,
If it fell to Earth, would it be found?

Shooting star up there,
We watch you as you fly,
How much further, for how much time,
Will you fly across our sky?

Nicola Morris (13)
King Henry VIII School

STAR SIGNS

Some people think star signs come true
And happen in real life
They say things like 'You're going to find love this week'
Or 'You're going to divorce your wife'!

Taurus, Aries and Gemini
They are some of the stars
The passages about them are quite silly
They are as silly as wooden cars!

You can ring up Mystic Meg if you want
And whisper down the phone
'What's going to happen to me this week?
Am I going to break a bone?'

All the stars have different logos
Gemini has two tall, terrific twins
Leo has a lion
And there are lots of other things!

Aquarius' logo is water
Water is a deep blue paradise
There are lots of different logos
They are all very nice!

I don't believe in star signs
I don't think they are true
Do you believe in star signs?
Do you? Do you? Do you?

Laura Copeland (13)
King Henry VIII School

ROMEO AND JULIET

They drew their swords and stepped into the road,
The servants were not at all mistaken.
The families were enemies of old
The war could end with lives being taken.
Romeo went to the party that night
Wearing a mask so he wouldn't be seen.
He was looking at other girls, in spite
Of pretending he was not very keen.
He crossed the hall and noticed Juliet,
Then decided he'd found his true love.
He thought and he thought and his mind was set
This girl was an angel sent from above.
The war forbade them to be together,
Made them keep their love silent for ever.

Laura Powell (13)
King Henry VIII School

FATE

All those planets moving around the solar system,
Do they really predict our fate
Or is what we say not true?
Does anyone know the truth?
Who made up these myths?
Why did they look at planets anyway?
Why do they look at stars?
Do planets' names mean things we do not know?
Are their shapes and sizes anything to go by?
Are their colours telling us anything we are to know?
Do the moons around these planets do anything to affect us?
Why are the planets there?

Sam Collins (13)
King Henry VIII School

THE SKY

One day I looked up very high,
I saw a small star in the sky.

It was shining very bright,
But then I saw a streak of light.

Was it a shooting star?
Was it a rocket car?

Was it my imagination,
Or was I singing - playing my PlayStation?

No of course not, it's a dream,
But I woke up with a gleam.

When I looked out I saw a stream of jet.

Craig Matthews (12)
King Henry VIII School

SPACE

When I see the stars twinkling in the sky,
I wonder if they're always there and then I wonder why,
I think about the astronauts looking down on Earth,
I wonder if they've always been there, ever since their birth,
Soon I see a shooting star, I wonder where they go,
To the end of the universe, travelling to and fro.
One day I would love to go up into space,
But I could never manage to leave the human race.

Rachel James (13)
King Henry VIII School

THE SIGN OF MY FAMILY

Zodiac signs are very clever,
I like to read mine every week,
My chosen sign would be a feather,
Because they are unique!

I am a Libra and like to be the boss,
I like to be the centre of attention.
Sometimes I get very cross,
And end up having a detention!

Cancer is the sign for my mum,
She's very loving and lots of fun.
The sign for Leo belongs to Dad,
Who at times can get very mad!

My little bro' he's an Aries,
Imaginative and away with the fairies,
Although he's generous and very kind,
He has a temper, so bare that in mind!

Jodie Malnati (11)
King Henry VIII School

CHRISTMAS

Christmas is about family greetings,
You also get a lot of presents,
It is lovely to see the Christmas tree,
The turkeys are lovely to taste.
When the Christmas lights are turned on
They are nice to see.
It's a lovely feeling on Christmas morning.

Tom Roberts (12)
King Henry VIII School

WAR

Bombs crash to the trenches
Pain turns to death,
Bullets fly from the guns.
Snipers fire at the SAS
Trench diggers freeze to death,
Planes get blown apart
Men get shot in the heart.
Women and children suffer
As their husbands and dads fight at war,
Babies and guns all over the floor.
War is at rest,
God bless.

Robert Pritchard (13)
King Henry VIII School

CRYSTAL CLEAR

Wall crusher
Side basher
Life saver
Welcoming passers
Calmly sways.

Mind twisting
Eyes whirling
So upsetting

Dusky grey
Muddy brown
Crystal clear.

Christy Collings (13)
King Henry VIII School

LOCKED OUT

Being locked out, is not really fun,
Especially if you're not in the sun.
When it's raining and pouring and no one's there,
The rain is falling right into your hair.

When you're waiting and waiting, but nobody arrives.
You're hungry and thirsty you don't know if you'll survive.
You wish and wish you hadn't lost your key
Your parents will get a key cut and make you pay the fee.

You've just come back from school and want to sit down
You're wondering if you should walk into town.
You look for a window that's open,
There aren't any, so you keep on hoping.

There's a car coming towards you, riding down the road,
It's a green colour that looks like a toad.
You're in the house now, out of the cold
Maybe you'll be able to keep your key one day when you're old.

Beth Kelly (12)
King Henry VIII School

STARS

When I look up in the sky
I look for a special star
One that shines and glitters
Down on me

I love the stars, they all look so pretty
It looks like someone has put them in place
There are lots of constellations
That come at different times of year

Astronomers look at them
And discover more about them
I don't see why
They're just patterns in the sky.

Rhian Auty (13)
King Henry VIII School

ZODIAC

The stars are bright in the midnight sky.
The moon is up so high, so high.
The people are now all in bed waiting for morning to come instead.
As they read their star signs this is how they go:

Pisces, the fish, splashing and playing.
Taurus, the bull, ranting and raving,
darting towards the big red target.
Scorpio, the scorpion, pinching and pecking
as it waddles across the sand.
Cancer, the crab, pinching across the soft, yellow sand.
Leo, the lion, roaring like thunder as it awakes from its sleep.
Aquarius, the water cold, calm and blue.
Aries, the ram butting and kicking its very hardest.
Gemini, the twins, the same but different.
Virgo, the mermaid, swimming and splashing.
Sagittarius, the archer, with his bow and arrow.
Capricorn, the goat, chewing and munching.
Libra, the scales, weighing and balancing.
These are the star signs in the sky,
so goodnight, goodbye, goodbye.

Roxanne Generalovic (13)
King Henry VIII School

THE FOUR SEASONS

The cold winter days
Snowballs flying
People crying

Children sleighing
I am playing

Frostbite infecting
Warm clothes are protecting

The spring sensation
Little lambs bleating
Whilst they're leaping

Over the stream
To the grass that's green

They're enjoying the fun
To the light of the sun

The luscious summer sun
I'm digging on my own
Before I go home

I'm having a swim in the sea
The yachts, the boats and me

I am in the car
The journey is so far.

The autumn breeze
The leaves are turning brown
And scattering all around

I am going mad because
Of my friend's dad

I am getting mean
In aid of Hallowe'en.

Neil Powell (11)
King Henry VIII School

GOLDILOCKS AND THE THREE BEARS

Over the hills and far away
A girl called Goldilocks
Came out to play.

She came to a house,
With a door open wide,
She was a cheeky girl,
So she stepped inside.

She found a bowl of porridge,
That wasn't too hot.
She was very hungry,
She ate the whole lot.

Soon she got tired,
And went upstairs,
She fell fast asleep,
But in came the three bears.

She jumped to her feet,
And ran to the door.
Sprinted away,
And was seen no more.

Emma Davies (11)
King Henry VIII School

FLOWERS

Flowers are red,
Flowers are white,
Flowers are gold,

They're beautiful,
Who gave them all?
God, He gave them all
I like flowers,
Especially the rose,
Because it smells so nice.

I like nature,
I like God,
Who gave God?
Nobody gave God.

Please God, please,
Give more flowers,
Especially the fragrant rose.

Priya Mohan (11)
King Henry VIII School

WINTER

When winter comes,
I shiver inside my house
Watching the last leaves fall off the trees.
Now it's cold nobody is out,
The season's come and go so soon,
Everywhere the ground is frozen
Rabbits are hibernating in their burrows,
Winter is coming.

Kashanie Tye (11)
King Henry VIII School

THE STAR SIGN FANTASY

They say 'You will find love this week',
But how are they supposed to know?
They read it in the planets and stars,
Somehow I don't think so.

Taurus, Scorpio, Cancer, Leo,
It's like a fashion trend,
People read them everywhere,
Will they ever end?

Strange, star symbols,
Different for each one,
A raging ram for Aries,
A goat for Capricorn.

Stars are little specks of dust,
Upon a carpet of black,
They leave as the sun comes up,
At night they come back.

Whoosh! There goes a shooting star,
It's flying past Mercury,
The planets also play a part
In the star sign fantasy.

But can they really tell your future,
Those dots up in the sky?
They tell you how your life will be,
And finally when you'll die.

Sarah Holder (13)
King Henry VIII School

STAR SIGNS

Virgo, the mermaid, her fin held high,
With curly, golden, cascading hair,
Elegant, graceful, she looks most divine.

Taurus, the charging bull, the red rag enrages him so,
He hurtles, angrily towards his target.

Cancer, the crab, crawling across the sand,
Watch out, watch out, or those pinchers might clamp.

Pisces, the fish, swimming along reasonably slow
Then darts so quickly where did it go?

Leo, the enormous, roaring lion, be on your guard,
He hasn't eaten for a while.

Libra, the scales, changing all the time,
Very rarely equal on both sides.

Scorpio, the deadly scorpion, its look tells you not to touch,
If you do, beware!

Sagittarius, the archer, armed with his bow and arrow
He sees his target, then he aims.

Capricorn, the goat, bleating on a far away hilltop
It grazes on mainly grass, or anything else that grows.

Aries, the ram, he has magnificent golden horns
If he meets another, it could mean headlocks till dawn.

Gemini, the twins, you never know which one is which
Until you look closely at the face.

Aquarius, flowing water, a glorious shade of blue
Travelling through streams, rivers, oceans, calm, rushing, rising,
It runs and runs, it never stops.

Amy Trinder (14)
King Henry VIII School

SCHOOLDAYS

Mondays

Monday's boring,
Early morning.
Back to work,
More homework.

Tuesdays

Not so bad,
But teacher's mad.
Music now,
My ears, 'Ow!'

Wednesdays

Teacher's hoarse,
Not children, of course.
Children bright and gay,
It's early finish day.

Thursdays

I like Thursday,
It's PE day.
Children are being rude,
Teacher's in a mood.

Fridays

Last day today,
Teacher's having another bad day.
New week next week
Head teacher's at his peak.

Robert Powell (11)
King Henry VIII School

DOLPHINS

Here come the dolphins,
Exploring the sea.

Leaping, twisting and jumping,
As they swim through the sea.

They dive to the bottom of the ocean,
Looking for their prey,
Very professionally.

They see,
The great, brightly coloured reefs,
Swaying gracefully.

What a fantastic sight,
Those intellectuals of the sea.

Becky Cochrane (12)
King Henry VIII School

DUMB BLONDE

There's nothing wrong with being blonde
Though airhead springs to mind
People say that fair means dumb and dippy
In fact you're just a peaceful hippy
And you're not a bimbo (all of the time)
We do have brains
And we're not insane
We can think for ourselves
We do like pink, but then so do Santa's elves.

Kayleigh Down (14)
King Henry VIII School

JETTING OFF

Jetting off to the stars
on a big spaceship,
oh I'd love to be with you
on your outer space trip.

10

Countdown has started

9

it's time to depart,

8, 7, 6, 5, 4, 3, 2, 1

All systems go

We lave lift-off!

Lewis Davies (11)
King Henry VIII School

TWELVE ZODIACS ON A TREE

Twelve zodiacs sitting on a tree,
out pops Leo, that means me!
Like to be the centre of attention,
Do anything to get there you
don't have to mention,
I'm bossy, but cool, I'm not a fool
Leo,
Leo,
That's me!

Laura Davies (11)
King Henry VIII School

LEO

My star sign is Leo,
I'm quite adventurous,
I am quite brave,
I'm not that strong,
I'm quite fierce,
I like reading,
I'm Leo the lion,
Well almost.

Jack Morse (11)
King Henry VIII School

ON THE WALL

Once I sat upon a wall and saw
A big feathery jackdaw.
He flew away and I saw the bird no more.
So when I sat upon a wall
I saw but nothing, nothing at all.

David Bishop (11)
King Henry VIII School

STAR

S   tar signs are interesting
T   hey tell a story of the stars
A   nd the planets from Earth to Mars
R   eally wicked they are.

Emily Williams (11)
King Henry VIII School

SCHOOL'S OUT

Trees sway
In the wind,
Silence.
Litter blows
Across the ground,
Silence.
Birds fly
Roof to roof,
Silence.
Heads down
Working, writing,
Silence.
Bell rings,
Pack away,
Chaos!

Natasha Williams (12)
King Henry VIII School

ZODIAC

Stars shining like twinkling eyes,
Floating around like occupied flies.
Planets revolving, I can't keep up,
Shooting stars landing in my cup.
Libra, Leo, Sagittarius and Scorpio,
Venus, Jupiter, Saturn and Pluto.
My eyes are blinded by the shining moon,
Sunset like the backside of a baboon.
Astronauts blasting into space,
Floating around this dark and lonely place.

Nesta Watkins (11)
King Henry VIII School

SLEEPOVER

One by one all taking care.
'Careful, mind, that's the noisy stair.'
'There's only one more stair to go.'
All of them walking on tiptoe.
The head girl looked around,
'Come on everyone! On the ground!'
Eight little girls crawling along the floor.
At last they had reached the great wooden door.
She put her hand on the handle and pulled it down.
All of the girls standing in their dressing gowns.
A creak occurred -
But was it heard?
Head girl's heart started thumping - boom, boom,
Would they ever get to the next room?
Got to the kitchen, headed towards the fridge,
Dodging the pet cat Midge,
Opened the fridge - a whoosh of cold!
Nothing there just a tomato covered in mould,
Looked at each other with disbelief,
Would they ever get to have a midnight feast?

Rosie Powell (11)
King Henry VIII School

ZODIAC SIGNS

Z   odiac is my poem, I'm about to tell
O   n a Taurus lies two sharp horns
D   ancing through the water is Pisces
I   n the sign of Leo is anger and rage,
A   ries the ram is hard and bossy,
C   ancer is a crab with big long pincers.

S tars make up some of the signs,
I n Aquarius is water carried away,
G emini twins are a loving sign,
N ewspapers tell us our fortunes,
S igns of the zodiac are great and fine.

Kate Jones (11)
King Henry VIII School

THE SEA

It's my first time at the sea today
It's big and blue and cold, they say,
And big waves break and flow away.
I can't wait to go to the sea today.

I'm in the car, and it comes to a halt,
I can smell a very strong smell of salt,
I realise with a sudden jolt
That I've arrived at the sea today.

I'm on the beach, I can see the waves,
Breaking, and rushing into nearby caves.
The surface is sparkling, from the sun's rays,
I'm standing near the sea today.

I'm close to the waves, they seem to hiss,
But I have prepared for this.
I enter, and it's sudden bliss!
I really love the sea today.

It's cold and blue and getting deep,
Into it I gladly leap.
The memory I will forever keep,
But now I must leave the sea today.

Hannah Burch (11)
King Henry VIII School

1 SOLAR SYSTEM AVENUE

Shooting stars pass the skies,
Then I stop and wonder why,
Stars are made of gases and rock
When they get old they burn out and die.
So now I know why
Venus is filled with plenty of love
Where as Mars doesn't even know
The meaning of the above.
Instead it's the red planet of hatred and war,
So Earth turns around and closes the door.
Jupiter and Saturn are greatest of friends,
They both have their own features.
Saturn has rings and Jupiter has spots
And to my knowledge *no creatures*
Uranus is a normal planet, a calming bluey colour
Pluto on the other hand is very much the same as Uranus.
Mercury is the hottest planet, but even better the sun
Is the hottest star in the entire universe
It lives in the same vicinity as the planets in the solar system,

Address = 1 Solar System Avenue.

Adele Morgan (11)
King Henry VIII School

SNOW

Serene, white snow,
falling from the sky
little children run about,
snowballs start to fly.

Children begin to cry,
gloves start to leak,
frostbite starts to sneak,
fingers start to weep.

Nathan Byrne (11)
King Henry VIII School

SECRET

My friend told me a secret,
A secret I mustn't let go,
I wanted to tell simply everyone -
But my friend said, 'Most definitely *no!*'

I thought about her secret,
Even when I was in bed,
I wanted to tell my mum,
But I kept it to myself instead.

I kept my friend's secret,
I didn't tell a soul,
I kept it for months and months
I was very good at it on the whole.

We went through school together
And then to university.
Then we had different jobs,
But she still lived next door to me.

We've both retired now,
We're both wrinkly and old,
But we still share her secret,
The secret I never told.

Mari Davies (11)
King Henry VIII School

SCHOOL

Here comes the bus
There goes the bell
Let's get ready to go
Up the stairs
Along the corridor
Through the door
Into class
Have you ever noticed
How school goes so fast?
Out of class
Through the corridor
Down the stairs
School seems to go so fast.

Hannah Goldsworthy (11)
King Henry VIII School

ANIMALS

Hedgehogs are prickly
Kittens are cuddly
They all have feelings.

Crabs are vicious
Ducks are delicious
They all have feelings

Some dogs are posh
Some are not
They all should be
Cared for in homes.

Eleanor Roberts (11)
King Henry VIII School

THE LIFE OF THE LIONESS

Out from the bush she comes.
Followed by fire, majesty and death.
She spots a gazelle grazing on the prairie,
Slink forward, low and deadly like a snake,
She slides, closer and closer, slower and slower.
Finally she springs, running and jumping,
In and out, around trees, around elephants,
Panting she stops and throws her head back,
And roars, bearing her fangs,
Others meet her, her family, her pride,
Little cubs dance around her, hungry and happy.
The master appears, expectantly for a meal,
She tries again successfully
She catches and kills.
Hungry, but shares,
With the will of nature by her side.

Kate Miles (11)
King Henry VIII School

HOROSCOPE

H   oroscopes determine whether your luck is good
O   r bad.
R   emember to check your horoscope,
O   n weekends when you're bored.
S   ome think horoscopes are the best thing since
C   able TV.
O   thers think they are rubbish,
P   eople have different opinions,
E   ven me!

Elin Jones (11)
King Henry VIII School

THE UNIVERSE

The universe is a wonderful thing,
so wonderful it makes people sing,
with the sun that shines so bright
and the moon that comes out at night.

The universe is a wonderful thing
so wonderful it makes people sing.
Friends and family which are always there,
that feed us food, fruit and sweets,
I just wish there was enough for everybody
to have a share.

The universe is a wonderful thing,
so wonderful it makes people sing.
Utopia - if there was such a thing,
we could live there together
in peace and harmony.

Helena Nilsson (11)
King Henry VIII School

WINTER FEELINGS

Walking through the cold, bare forests,
squirrels snuggled up all warm and cosy.
Hibernation time for the great, black bear.
Children on their bright red sledges.
Minute speckles of snow falling to the soft, white ground,
cats and dogs inside, scratching and scraping at the shiny windows.
Mum's in the kitchen making spongy, warm cakes.
At tea time there will be empty dishes.
Dad's in the living room watching the weather forecast.
Lots more snow tomorrow!
The children all shout for joy!

Sarah Dobbins (11)
King Henry VIII School

The Moon

The moon is shining bright,
And I can see its face at night.
I wonder why it stares at me,
And what it really thinks of me.

The sky is dark and frightful,
But there's nothing more delightful,
Than the moon in all its glory,
Its face could tell a story.

But no one knows who put it there,
Or why it's there.
We just don't have a clue,
But still it watches over you.

Katie McCarthy (11)
King Henry VIII School

The Zodiac

Our lives are planned by the stars,
That twinkle like bright diamonds
And planets solid deep as rock,
All from the secret imaginary belt of the zodiac,
Deep, dark, dingy days,
Or light, long, lazy days
Are all gifts from above,
The crazy Cancer or scary Scorpio
To name just a few,
We read our stars everyday
And hope we have time to play.

Arwyn Woodford (13)
King Henry VIII School

DOGS

Dogs chew your shoes
When or whose
Does not matter
They just get fatter.

When the lid rattles
It sounds like a herd of cattle
It means walk
So we can talk.

When they bark
In the dark
They keep us awake
Like an earthquake.

Some are nasty,
They can eat your pastie
So don't leave it on the side
Or you mouth will be wide.

Katie Lias (12)
King Henry VIII School

ARGUING

Arguing is like
people who can't sing.

It's horrible when people argue,
it's a bit like a war, but no guns.

It's like a devil has got in
their brain and won't get out.

It's like there is nothing right.

Rachel Gooding (11)
King Henry VIII School

ZODIAC

All the planets surrounded by stars,
Jupiter, Uranus, Venus and Mars,
I love Saturn and its rings,
Bits and bobs and shiny things,
Around the planets lies the man in the moon,
There he stands in his spacesuit cocoon,
Like a rocket the stars are shooting,
As they race the owls are tooting,
As kids look out to say 'Goodnight'
The planets are such a magnificent sight,
All the planets and stars go to bed,
As sleepy children nod their heads.

Chloe Williams (11)
King Henry VIII School

THINGS THAT GO BUMP IN THE NIGHT

When you are asleep in bed
Ghosts pick at your pillows,
Try on your clothes,
Play with your toys,
Pull off your blankets,
And eat toast
At the end of your bed.
They leave crumbs,
All over the floor,
But at the first sign of day
They fly away!

Kimberly Jones (11)
King Henry VIII School

MY POEM

A single shaft of shimmering light,
glints malevolently on the defiant blade of a dagger!
Beneath a tranquil moon a lake ripples a silent rhythm,
glistening and fragmented like shattered diamonds.
My dog gazing innocent and so vulnerable,
enticing me to obey his every command.
A battered, dilapidated leather purse,
clenched in my father's immense fist.
Stumbling aimlessly up a forbidding mountain,
contemplating over past regrets.
Subtle caressing whispers, echo ever constant in my thoughts,
gentle words conjured by the truth of true love . . .
Universe entwined with a mortal soul,
united for eternity in a great, big bowl!

Rachael Hughes (13)
Monmouth Comprehensive School

WIND

Lightly blowing as a breeze,
But then turns to make us freeze.
Ferocious as a lion's bite,
But kids still go to fly their kite.
Rapidly moving like the sea,
Humming calmly like a bee.
There's nothing at all that you can do,
Wish and wish all night through.
But when it comes to a new day,
The wind will decide its own way!

Sara Garrett (11)
Monmouth Comprehensive School

A SPINNING WORLD AND A TURNING MOON

A foreign letter,
written in the hand of Alemnshe,
the photo of my old classmates,
as memories swell back.
The birthday card from Jo,
still thoughtfully scribbled.
A very special person,
and the warm smile they gave.
The brightest star,
a dancing pixie in black
and the sunset that fell
over my favourite beach.
All happens as the world spins
and the moon turns round.

Claire Tremlett (13)
Monmouth Comprehensive School

TOFFEE

Toffee is my hamster, he is a cheeky chap,
He's honey-coloured all over his back.
Always hungry, in the night he's running
Around his cage, or going round and round
In his exercise wheel, biting on his salt block,
Or trying to wake me up by biting on the cage
And hanging off the top and falling off.
His cage has three floors,
The first for sleeping and playing,
Second for eating and drinking,
Last of all the third floor is for exercising
And where he bites his salt block.

Chloe West (11)
Monmouth Comprehensive School

THE UNIVERSE

The universe is always expanding at enormous rates,
New exciting planets created all the time,
The stuffed turkey cooked for a fabulous Christmas lunch,
Suddenly lays a round, spotty egg,
It plummeted and smashed into the shiny model spaceship,
Yolk flies everywhere splatterin' walls and the ceiling,
Tommy G wildly drank all the contents of the beer barrel,
He did it the night before, he now has a humungous hangover,
He wears his tattered spacesuit with pride,
It's launch day and he still has a bangin' headache,
He enters the shuttle, the pressure is intense,
The shuttle lifts off, it feels like it will snap at any moment,
Finally their destination, silent space.
This is where no one can hear you scream for help!

Tom Garwood (13)
Monmouth Comprehensive School

COMING HOME FROM WORK

Chattering and scuffling,
Crowding all around me,
I glance up at the evening sky.
The buildings towering over me.
Exhausted, I turn a corner,
More factories, more people,
Darkness closing in on me.
The smoky streets of Salford Narrow,
My children greet me.

Michaela Painter (11)
Monmouth Comprehensive School

IN THE BAG

A bag, everything that makes me, in this bag . . .
A blood stain, only reminder of a hard year's work
Trickles slowly to the base.
A necklace reminding me of a lost friend,
Living forever in our memories.
This pack of cigars, all ready to be burnt,
Obviously oblivious of their fate.
This ego is James', it bulges and swells,
Never finding anything better than itself.
These people who patronise me, locked up forever,
Never to talk down to me again.
Tears of a loved one, dripping slowly down,
I'll never let them feel so sad again.
So many things, such a short life to admire them in.

Mathew Willcock (13)
Monmouth Comprehensive School

TEDDY

I have a teddy that stays with me,
He does what I do, he sees what I see.

My teddy is big, fluffy and white,
And he stays with me all through the night.

In the morning when I open my eyes,
My teddy sits there, big and wise.

And before I go to school each day,
I say to my teddy, 'We will soon play.'

I have a teddy that stays with me,
He does what I do, he sees what I see.

Katie Small (12)
Monmouth Comprehensive School

WHAT AM I?

I am a twinkle in a child's eye,
I am a piece of broken glass glowing by.
My friends help to brighten up the sky,
I am a night-time torch for you and I.

I am an egg yolk submerged in a blue sea,
I am a yellow smudge on a crystal blue sheet.
Obscured by the moon from time to time,
Reflecting my smile on the Earth.

People say I'm full of cheese,
And land on me as they please.
I have been once in a cartoon movie,
I influence the tides on distant shores.

I am a piece of blue, white and green pâpier maché.
Many people survive off me,
A source of life to vast civilisations,
Rotating and spinning, locked in space.

Rebecca Couchman (11)
Monmouth Comprehensive School

MEN AT WAR

The heavy boots that the soldiers wore,
Marching for miles on end,
But now and again,

They would come across the bodies of
Their fellowmen.

The jackets they wore that kept them warm,
What brave men who fought in the war.

Joe Waters (11)
Monmouth Comprehensive School

SAINT DAVID'S DAY - A DREAM COUNTRY

Wales is a lovely place,
It puts a smile on everyone's face.
The dragons flying in the sky,
In the clouds way up high.

Daffodils are flowers with trumpets,
They are as yellow as buttered crumpets.
Leeks are vegetables of white and green,
They are a symbol of David that you all have seen.

Welsh ladies and lovely Welsh cakes,
Beautiful rivers and beautiful lakes.
We all join in the celebration
That's going on throughout the nation!

Oh Wales is a lovely place,
It's full of beauty and of grace.

Amy Phillips (11)
Monmouth Comprehensive School

MY JOURNEY

I walk across the road so cold
Listening to the birds up high,
And the cars speeding by.

Across the road so busy,
Into the wood so cold and bare,
One little bird flickers
And the noise echoes into the trees.

The sound of the cars fading away,
This is where I want to be.

Kayleigh Brown (12)
Monmouth Comprehensive School

MY JOURNEY TO THE MOON

My journey to the moon was exciting.
I took off from America in a top of the range spaceship.
We were travelling at lightning speed.
There was a little window by the side of me that I could look out of.
When we took off it was hard to see,
But when we got into space it was easier to see because we were
                                                    going slower.

When I first saw the moon,
On Earth it was noon.
My face just lit up,
And I shut up.
The first expression I got was amazement,
I had never seen anything like it before.
As I stepped out of the rocket and my feet touched the ground
I realised that I was walking the slowest I had ever walked.
I only had a few hours on the moon,
Then I got back into the rocket for a safe journey home.

Michael Cleaves (12)
Monmouth Comprehensive School

THE BOAT TRIP

My feet are wet and going flip, flop,
The weight of my shoes is weighing me down,
My toes are all squashed up at the bottom of my shoes,
My hands are clinched around the oars,
My arms are getting tired with the back and fore action,
My ears are cold and wet because of the rain,
I can hear seagulls circling in the air,
My nose is red with cold,
I can see lots of undiscovered islands,
I see the sun start to set.

Matthew Harvey (13)
Monmouth Comprehensive School

MY ATLAS

This watch was worn
by my great uncle, now dead.

New Zealand lies in two parts
one has cities, one empty.

The beach of my dreams
sand and more sand.

When I was small, a stranger
gave me a teddy.

The model plane I brought on holiday,
it gives me good luck.

The big atlas my mum brought,
it helps me to get around.

When I shut my bag
I realised it was all a dream.

Thomas Emblen (14)
Monmouth Comprehensive School

JOURNEY TO LANZAROTE

My feet: I have trainers on and my feet are cramped in an aeroplane.

My hands: I have a newspaper and my hands are hot.

My ears: The noise from the aeroplane and engines.

My nose: I can smell oil like there is oil leaking.

My eyes: I look out the window and I can see a lot of clouds.

Simon Morris (12)
Monmouth Comprehensive School

TRAVELLING IN OUTER SPACE

My big shoes are lime green and glittery; I am riding on a
really fast electric bike. My laces are bright pink; my feet
are flying through the air in outer space.

My hands are in my bright yellow gloves. I am
pressing lots of buttons on my electric bike; my
hands are all sweaty inside.

My headphones cover my ears; my ears are red all
over from the cold in the air. My ears are picking
up lots of noises like beeping on the buttons.

My nose is very cold. I can smell the exhaust on
my bike. I can also smell the air from around as I
travel through the air.

My eyes are covered with my purple goggles, to stop
the smoke from getting in them. I can see lots of planets
and stars, as I am whizzing past them on my bike.

Sophie Jones (12)
Monmouth Comprehensive School

FAIRY GARDEN

At the bottom of the garden
It's a very special place,
It's full of little fairies
But you never see their face.

They dance around in sunlight
And sit on mushroom stools.
If they get a little hot
They swim in forest pools.

It's a very pretty sight
That not many people see.
I don't share them with my friends,
I keep them all for me.

When the sun goes down at night
And they quietly fly away,
I go to bed with my dreams
That they'll come another day.

Cassie Jones (11)
Monmouth Comprehensive School

MY JOURNEY

I'm wearing tough walking boots
Made of hard leather,
I feel relaxed and comfortable wearing them.

I am sweaty and hot moving about in this heat,
My hands feel heavy carrying this rucksack on my back,
The heat is burning the back of my neck.

I can hear the noises of different creatures,
The motor roaring in this vehicle,
The gravel being crushed by the wheels.

I can smell a horrible odour from the van,
The animal's droppings.

I can see the animals running out on the grounds,
The amazing sunset in the distance,
And the stars shining over the African prairie.

Jessica Davies (12)
Monmouth Comprehensive School

MY JOURNEY

Pushing off the ground
In my soft padded shoes,
Slightly worn down on left shoe
From ollieing on my skateboard.

My hands covered in small blisters
From grabbing hold of my deck,
Doing lots of air tricks
Down the park with my friends.

My ears are red and hot,
My beanie keeps them warm.
The ring in my left ear
Catches in my hat.

The graze on my nose is healing,
Not so sore as it was
When I bailed out on the street course
And fell flat on my face.

My eyes have contact lenses in,
White with black dot in the middle,
All I can see in front of me
Is the massive street course.

David Thomas (12)
Monmouth Comprehensive School

DEEP, DEEP DOWN

Splashing up and down go my feet in
the deep blue murky sea.

My hands are circling my face
frantically in front crawl.

I can hear the bobbing of boats on the
surface and the splash of the waves.

I can smell the fish when they go by
in swarms and the salt water.

I can see dolphins jumping in and out of
the sea and fish going by in swarms,
all in the bluish colour of my goggles.

Kerry Louise Jones (12)
Monmouth Comprehensive School

MY JOURNEY TO SLEEP

I sit and watch the bright TV,
Then suddenly my eyes close slowly.
I slither upstairs, I'm getting tired,
My eyes are a blur, I've lost my room!

My brother scares me,
I run down the stairs at 50mph,
The wind rushes on my face,
My eyes start to shut once more.

I slide up the stairs
Dragging my tired feet,
I see my bed, it's fresh and crisp,
The room's full of shadows, I want to sleep.

I get into bed, it feels cold,
I can't get to sleep, I count sheep,
I find myself sliding into a glorious dream.

The next thing I know the sunlight gleams
Into my eyes like drops,
I lie there awake until I must get up,
Then school begins.

Danielle Lewis (12)
Monmouth Comprehensive School

THE JOURNEY

Jumping out of bed, looking forward to the week ahead,
Have a quick breakfast and jump into the shower,
Packing all our suitcases, hoping they will close,
Saying goodbye to our houses, not seeing them for a week,
Our dogs look up at us with a worried face,
'Aren't we coming with you?' rushes through their minds.

Put our suitcases in a pile under the town hall,
Sit outside the Angel Inn with the smell of curry very strong,
We all climb onto the coach,
All of us twelve children smiling, laughing and handfuls of sweets
                                                        on our laps,
People waving goodbye to us, cameras clicking.
Driving along all the small country roads but the motorway soon
                                                        meets us.

Arrive at Manchester Airport with aeroplanes flying over us,
We put our suitcases onto a trolley and enter the giant building.
'Ding-dong, flight BD4537 to Corfu is delayed for six hours.'
We all give a big sigh and move forward in the queue,
We finally reach the desk and wave goodbye to our treasured suitcases,
We all head off to find a seat,
And split up to have a bite to eat and go shopping in the few shops,
We all meet back up as we enter the departure lounge.

We all tried to get to sleep on the long rows of comfy chairs,
When over the radio it said, 'Ding-dong, flight BD4537 to Corfu,
Please can all people go to the final gate.'
We all let out a little cheer and walked to gate number 11,
We all stood in a long queue and clambered aboard the plane,
I sat down and put my seat belt on and the big engine started,
It slowly moved around the airport passing giant planes,
And then suddenly took off, my head was pinned against the seat.
It soon slowed down and it gently glided along on top of the world.

Out of the small, little window we could see the top of the French Alps,
Like little sand ripples down by the water's edge,
We could see the early morning sun glinting on the sea as we landed
                                                       at Corfu airport.
Lastly we stepped out into the warmth of the Greek sun.

Ellie Cull (12)
Monmouth Comprehensive School

JOURNEY TO THE FRIDGE

Wake up in the middle of the night,
Try to get back to sleep, but can't.
I wonder what's in the fridge,
Climb out of bed in a trance,
Fall over my school bag,
That woke me up proper,
And some dirty plates,
I knew I should have tidied my room.
Get to the top of the stairs,
Hold on to the banister for dear life.

Somehow reach the kitchen door,
Open it and there's something
Moving towards me, it licks my hand,
Stupid me, only the dog.

Open the fridge and grab anything,
Shove it in my mouth,
Urgh! Old, mouldy sandwich!
Wash mouth out with water,
Won't chance it again, going back to bed.
Walk across the room and fall over the dog.

Anna Mackenzie (12)
Monmouth Comprehensive School

THE HIDDEN TRUTH

Nothing was really real,
The truth was just covered up by silk lining,
Screaming and tearing at the leather walls,
The truth would soon be free,
The passport was a lying identity,
It belonged to the man who didn't own the bag,
The diary was disturbing,
Its last entry was never finished,
Nobody heard the gun shot,
Only the people who were not his friends,
The fear of being found out had gone,
For he had been found out,
As the bag, tarred, colourless and empty,
Mocked his extinguished life.

Louise Kulbicki (13)
Monmouth Comprehensive School

PASSING SHADOW

He slinks through the shadows
To where he would lie,
Along a now darkened alleyway,
Passing under the road where memories loomed.
Beneath the old, gnarled oak
He makes one last leap over a dry stone wall
To his final resting place.
No longer the proud champion of his race,
No glimmer in his eyes,
He rests his head on a cracked gravestone
Never to stir again.

Steven Cresswell (13)
Monmouth Comprehensive School

COLOURS OF MY MIND

Fiery, angry red, devouring up the lives of war-torn lands.
Thin, light blue, fading away with the lives of starving children.
Sickly green for envy and jealousy of hardworking,
deserving people in the world.

Gold for the gallant heroes of old, fighting for valour.
Slimy treachery like a slithery silver snake.
Bright, happy, ecstatic, radiant yellow, like the sunlight.
Coal-black like a raven to signify an empty death.
A white mist to shroud the terror and the scream.
The colossal forests, green as emeralds.
Dark orange, as angry as the stripes of a ferocious tiger.
A royal colour, purple, but deadly too.
Glittering silver, the universe and the future.

Simon Brown (11)
Monmouth Comprehensive School

MY SPECIAL PLACE

A large, grey barn with chalky stone walls and a fragile roof,
Bales upon bales of dark, scratching straw,
A huge vehicle with monster wheels and settled dust,
A small, wooden hutch with a sand-coloured rabbit
scratching and nibbling,
The distant squabble of hens and fluttering feathers,
A pile of unwanted stones lay in the corner, cold and grey,
The soothing purr from a silky, soft cat,
Ice-cold hands shaking and turning red with the
blood rush of warmth,
Hours of laughter and silliness with friends,
That's my special place.

Poppy Roberts-Tudhope (11)
Monmouth Comprehensive School

SPRING

Green shoots appear from below,
Sweet scents of flowers are on the airflow.
Newly born lambs prance here and there
While most animals crawl out of their winter lair.
Cows graze on the farm,
The winter won't have done any harm.
Flowers look beautiful up the lane
As the lush grass blades are not in winter's prison of cold pain.
Fox cubs stay in their mother's care
As newly hatched chicks breathe their first air.
My favourite flowers grow through March, April and May
As graceful horses eat their hay.
Spring is colourful and bright,
I think spring is a wonderful sight.

Katie Hopkins (11)
Monmouth Comprehensive School

MY SPECIAL PLACE

My special place is behind my house.
It has tall trees and bushes,
The bushes are filled with blackberries,
There is a fence which my friends and I try and get over,
There's a little forest with a stream running through it,
With big rocks and stepping stones.
The place is full of grass and trees,
Ahead is an alleyway, dark and gloomy, full of mud,
That leads to a close where my friend lives.
Blackbirds fly around at the blackberries.
Nearby is a very steep slope that we try and run down,
But we always manage to fall over.
So that is my special place.

Susannah Browning (11)
Monmouth Comprehensive School

THE BRILLIANT BAG

The Great Barrier Reef
with all its beauty and treasures, fish and sharks.
The Amazon forest with all its secrets and animals
taking the stitches out one by one.
Volcanoes with all their power and glory
bursting out the top of the bag.
Watching the movies I have watched before
in a flexible wallet cinema.
A mobile phone so I can contact anybody,
anywhere in my own telephone box.
A fountain pen, to write what I see around me.
This bag is out of this world,
but includes part of our own world.

Rhys James (13)
Monmouth Comprehensive School

THE BAG OF DREAMS

An old silver framed picture of a little girl
An old leather journal locked away
The gold elephant pendant
The mountains hidden deep in the forest
Sunshine shining through my window
A voice of a friend that seems almost forgotten
A picture of a little girl in a silver frame
An old black journal locked away in the darkness
The gold elephant pendant trembled in the old lady's hands
The mountains screaming 'freedom' were hidden in the forest
Sunshine shone through my rose-tinted window
A friend's voice called out, that seems almost forgotten . . .

Samantha Davies (13)
Monmouth Comprehensive School

THE TREK TOWARDS THE JUNGLE!

I'm wearing dance shoes, they are made out of the finest material, smooth and satin, shiny, elasticated straps. They allow my feet to point, little steps I take, hardly making a noise, quickly and quietly moving.

I look down, my hands are clenched, colourful nails are hidden by the palm of the hand, they are cool, cold and clammy, they move as I run faster, barely any wrinkles cover them.

My ears, they are pierced with two jewels, turquoise blue in colour. I hear growls, sweet singing from birds. I recognise which ones, larks, robins, starlings and the owl. I am aware of every sound!

My nose is pale pink and smothered in freckles, it bobs up and down, up and down again and again! I can smell unusual smells out here in the jungle! Sweet, moist, strong and faint. Different smells and familiar ones. They remind me of so many things!

My mouth is closed, teeth gripping the sides of my lips. I am concentrating hard! My lips are dry, rough as well! My pointy tongue edges to the corner of my lips. Scarlet, as red as my strap upon my shoe. I open my mouth to scream as lions are chasing me, but no sound comes out.

Carla Morgan (12)
Monmouth Comprehensive School

KING OF THE VIEW

White coated men with offensive weapons
Offering balls to the king of the view.
The sudden burst of a smear on the painting
Causes the crowd to cheer.
The body of stone is being worshipped by the
Giant conifers making the border,
Making it impossible for an easy escape.

Gabrielle Couchman (11)
Monmouth Comprehensive School

ENCHANTMENT IN A BAG

The last diamond ring
fell from a lonely finger,
the trees whispered
between the misty leather,
the twig burned
in the forest fire,
my friends laughed
on a gloomy day,
the whisker fell
from my cat's fluffy face,
the footsteps walked
between the cotton stitchings,
the small, leather bag
held enchantment throughout.

Hannah Morris (13)
Monmouth Comprehensive School

THE ONE

The first time I met you
It was love at first sight,
But as time went by
All we did was fight.
My heart is for you,
I couldn't say no,
But when you left me standing,
I had to let go.
My friends knew it was wrong,
But my faith in you stayed strong.
Even now that we're apart
You will always remain in my heart.

Karis Jones (13)
Monmouth Comprehensive School

MY CATS

Sooty,
sleek and velvety
when curled on my bed asleep.
She is a *tyrannosaurus rex*
to shrews, moles and voles
when hunting.
I love the way
she cleans her face with her paws.
Elegantly licking
with her
rough tongue.

KitKat,
furry and fluffy,
an innocent,
sweet baby
when asleep
on a chair.
He is a
stripy, fierce tiger
from the Amazon jungle.
I love cuddling him.
His purr
is like a drum beating
rhythmically.

Rebecca Jones (11)
Monmouth Comprehensive School

SADNESS!

As I look across the deserted fields, trees sway violently,
The sky forms great plumes of cloud,
The air turns vicious and agitated,
My stomach begins to twist and turn,
I hear the noise.

My whole body trembles,
I close my eyes in anguish,
I clench my fists,
My muscles start twitching,
I see the white coats in the field.

Emma Powell (13)
Monmouth Comprehensive School

MY AMAZING TRIP

I'll try to make this short an' snappy
I thought you'd like to know
I went on an amazing trip
Long, long ago!

I went somewhere called Cacca Coo
It was such an amazin' place
I got to see a load of animals
And stayed with my friend called Grace!

Can I say that Cacca Coo
Is in space, on a big dog's poo!

At Cacca Coo I saw,
An upside down bird,
It was so absurd!
A tiny elephant
And I taught it to chant!

I saw a blue, sparkly fish
I said 'Capish' and it vanished!
A huge, weird bug,
And it gave me a hug!

Then I said goodbye,
And all the animals started to cry.

Alicia Phelps (11)
Monmouth Comprehensive School

THE ROOKIE

I must carry my life in my bag,
For fear my secret, to be discovered.

I keep running away from my pastimes,
I keep running away from my secrets.

In my sports bag I carry a mountain,
An extinct volcano, never again to erupt.

I killed my son and decapitated him
And his severed head lies there in a bag.

I killed him with a kitchen knife,
Used for shredding animal carcasses,

And I stole from him,
His mobile phone,

For my own personal use . . .

Christopher Were (13)
Monmouth Comprehensive School

STORM

The storm darkens the sky like the eclipse,
Driving bolts of lightning to the ground like a nose-diving plane.
Thunder bellows like an ox's pounding footsteps on solid mud.
The screaming winds sound like a dying banshee screaming for
one last time.

Creaking trees bend like they have no end, swinging like
elasticated dreams.
Spirals of grass twirling and spinning forever until the wind dies
Like a rabbit caught by a scheming falcon's talons.
The sky opens like a baby with a new toy and the air is tranquil.

Sam Williams (11)
Monmouth Comprehensive School

WARM MEMORIES

Emeralds encrusting
My sweet silver pillbox.
The priceless gem
I found upon a moonlit beach.
My grandmother's pendant
Lies musty, alone.
Shimmering stardust
That fell from the sky.
Silky-white cobwebs
That glisten in the sun.
The lonely songbird
Fluttering high in the trees.
The warmth in my heart
As I delve into memories.

Deborah Brewis (13)
Monmouth Comprehensive School

THE MOVE

The rain trickled down boringly,
The city was a blurred picture on the horizon.
As the car speeded along
the wheels sloshed through the puddles.
The country road was bumpy
and all they could see was hundreds of smooth, green meadows.
The radio sang out dully, with the odd crackle.
The lane narrowed and became overgrown with hedgerows.
They turned into the long drive.
The sound of gravel crunching underneath them
met their ears.
The grand house stood tall and proud
waiting for them.

Rhoslyn Lawton (12)
Monmouth Comprehensive School

A JUNGLE JOURNEY

Through the bushes I saw the sun glisten,
I heard a noise and stopped to listen.

The noise was of a jaguar creeping,
Then I caught a small monkey peeping.

I saw a bird swoop to the ground,
Then I looked to see what it had found.

The breaking twigs below my feet,
Alerted a snake I didn't want to meet.

Lightning struck and a branch did crack,
The rain went through my waterproof mac.

Then I smelt the rotting trees,
Standing proud among the dancing leaves.

Biting insects in my hair
Was getting too much to bear.

In the gloom, all alone,
All I wanted to see was home.

Ginette Campbell (12)
Monmouth Comprehensive School

FARMERS

Farmers plough their stubbled fields,
Lorries fetch last year's yields.

Farmers check their sheep on quads,
And by their side are their sheepdogs.

Farmers plant next year's crops
Hoping that they won't be flops.

Farmers go and cut their hedges,
And make some hay with flat 8 sledges.

Farmers cut their wheat with a combine,
'This crop looks just fine.'

Daniel Cornish (13)
Monmouth Comprehensive School

A JOURNEY

The bell has gone, I pack up to leave,
Oh crikey, look! I've got ink on my sleeve.

Pushing and shoving, there's no time to care,
As hundreds of bodies run down the stairs.

I race for the bus, has it gone? No, not yet,
The driver's impatient, he's tapping his fingers I bet.

I climb on board and find somewhere to sit,
I'm huffing and puffing, I must be unfit.

We're finally off, we're finally free,
I hope we get there quickly, I want to watch TV.

Round the bends and up the hill,
If he drives much faster, I'm going to be ill.

Here's the first stop, some friends say goodbye,
The doors close again with a mechanical sigh.

Next stop now is for my sister and me,
At the bus shelter that is under a tree.

We wave and shout, 'Cheerio and farewell,
We'll see you tomorrow at the sound of the bell.'

Sam McCoy (12)
Monmouth Comprehensive School

The Girl Of Wishes

Sunset glows and moonlight flickers still,
Fiery balls burn billions of midnight galaxies away.
A shooting star I wish upon
To make my dreams come true.

A white horse of princess elegance
Glides across the chill night air,
Fluttering behind a satin handkerchief
Of purest innocence.

A crown of ocean pearl
Sits daintily upon fair silk hair,
Softly whips around her snow white face.

A rose of scarlet red,
Blooms of luscious perfume in a white lace dress,
As the eve of moonlight dies,
Dawn flies past.

Tiger hot, the wishes of angels
Fade slowly away.
A shooting star I wished upon
To make my dreams come true.

April Chambers (11)
Monmouth Comprehensive School

The Seasons

In summer the sun shines bright,
So children play on the beach until night.

In autumn the leaves turn from green to brown,
Then they fall to the ground.

In winter everyone wraps up warm,
And sing carols to the break of dawn.

In spring buds pop from the trees and ground,
Where there's always new life around.

Danielle Homer (11)
Monmouth Comprehensive School

LONELINESS

You know what it feels like
When you're all alone,
Your mind tends to drift off
As if into the unknown.

You look up and wonder
What's beyond the sky,
That's when the loneliness hits you
And you just can't help but cry.

There's no one there to talk to,
No one to hold your hand,
You feel just like a pebble
Upon a beach of sand.

No birds in the sky,
No fish in the sea,
I look into the water
To see someone looking at me.

I do not like this feeling,
When will it go away?
I wish someone was here,
Someone who's here to stay.

Sasha Hiscock (14)
Monmouth Comprehensive School

THINGS IN MY BAG

Here in my bag are items I have kept like;

A sepia photograph taken of a sailor,
who was lost at sea.

The bright Venus,
fell from the sky above.

The tropical rainforest of South America,
flourish in the dark depths of the leather world.

The friendship of a friend,
fills the bag with happiness.

Here is sand dredged from my holiday,
bringing memories and joy.

'I love you'
said by someone I know.

These things I will treasure forever!

Rachael McCoy (13)
Monmouth Comprehensive School

SUMMER HOLIDAY

As the days go rushing by
I wake up early, in bed I lie.
See the sun go from east to west,
Hear the robin singing with his redbreast.
Leaves are coming on the trees,
Hear the sound of buzzing bees.

See the ponies grazing in the field,
Ice lolly box definitely not sealed.
As the kittens play around
Pepsi barking, not an unusual sound.
As school comes around the corner
I'm sure my school shoes have got much smaller!

Claire Hope (11)
Monmouth Comprehensive School

THE TIDE

White horses rushing towards the beach
Where fishermen try to catch fish.

The waves are crashing against the cliffs,
The surf spraying right up to the sky.

Rock pools are slowly filling up,
Covering the starfish which stick to the rocks.

Surfers try to ride the waves,
Skimming their boards across the top.

Crabs biting toes, people saying, 'Ouch'.
Crabs trying to walk but getting swept away.

Shells are scattered along the shore,
Brightly coloured and shining in the sun.

The tide is in and at the end of the day
People go home tired and happy.

Abigail Gwilliam (11)
Monmouth Comprehensive School

MY HALLOWE'EN HORROR!

On Hallowe'en
I was dressed like a queen,
I fell in a ditch
And looked like a witch!

Me an' my mates went to 'Trick or treat?'
To get a chocolate bar or maybe a sweet,
On the way I saw a pumpkin
That had the face of an ugly goblin!

As I went home
I spotted a gnome,
That jumped up and down
And showed me his frown!

Then during the night
I had a fright,
I awoke to find the Devil
And to my astonishment his name was Neville!

Siân Knapman (11)
Monmouth Comprehensive School

DREAMS COME TRUE

A secret which someone special told me.
The photos of friends,
Who had fun.
The CD that played
Every single song.
The silent scream echoes
Between the leather walls.

The hands that clapped, clapped
Very fast.
All my friends sneered
And cheered.
My special bag,
Which makes my dreams come true.

Sarah Meredith (14)
Monmouth Comprehensive School

IN THE BAG

A brown leather bag,
I wonder what's inside . . .
A wooden box,
Carved beautifully.
A locket of hair,
Brown and plaited.
My old black cat,
I used to adore him.
A month old lottery ticket,
One I'd love to give to a tramp.
When I was younger
I was given a very special bracelet,
To which I lost and now found,
After expecting a world of wonder
The bag is filled full of emptiness
Oh well, life goes on . . .

Sam Coffey (14)
Monmouth Comprehensive School

JOURNEY

On
to the
deck I run
I wave frantically
to my mum
My tears are streaming
as I am leaving
'Hello!' I hear from behind
As I turn around I find
an old friend of mine
We were mates when I was nine
We go to tea together, we talk about old times
and how we used to make up silly little rhymes
We had a joke, we had a laugh
We remembered our old
homes in Bath
The anchor drops low
I have to go
I'll always remember
that special friend
and the times
we spent
together.

Robyn Fletcher (12)
Monmouth Comprehensive School

MY WINTER POEM

It was a cold winter's morning,
The ground was crisp with frost,
We went for a stroll in the countryside
And ended up completely lost.

Staying calm we tried to find a way home,
But hours went by and we were chilled to the bone.
Eventually we stumbled across an old country lane
Which allowed us to find our way home again.

Lisa Meek (12)
Monmouth Comprehensive School

MY JOURNEY AS A SHELL

I start my life fixed to a rock,
Then the waves hit and give me a shock,
Suddenly my whole life is prised away,
And in the rough surf I bob and sway.
All around me are other moving creatures,
Swimming around with bright coloured features,
Back and forth the tide swirls me about,
Until a large wave spits me out.
Now all alone I lie on the sand,
When swiftly I am grasped by a human hand,
My pearly shape is touched by a finger,
Then the person moves on and doesn't linger.
I am placed in a bucket with other shells,
Bits of seaweed and more salty smells,
I am jostled about as the bucket is swung,
And wonder what my destiny will become.
I am carefully washed and placed in a flower bed,
Surrounded by trees, grass and garden shed,
Each day I am warmed by the rays of the sun,
And gentle moonbeams when the day is done.
I no longer hear the harsh sounds of the sea,
Just a solitary bird tapping its beak on me.

Lara Craig (12)
Monmouth Comprehensive School

SEASONS

Come spring the fields are all green,
The cows and calves everywhere are to be seen.
The birds are busy building nests,
The cuckoo in the tree rests.

Summer days are warm and sunny,
The bees from their hives are gathering honey.
With sunny spells and showers of rain
The fields of corn become full of golden grain.

Autumn turns the leaves reddish-brown,
In the wind and rain they fall down.
The fields are all brown and bare,
It is easy to see rabbit and hare.

In winter down on the farm
The cows and calves feed in the barn.
The hedgerow's covered in berries and seeds
For all the birds to feed.

Trevor Bowen (13)
Monmouth Comprehensive School

MIGRATION

The journey starts,
In lines and charts,
Wings all beating,
Small hearts floating.

We fly all day and all night,
When it's dark we end our flight,
Not much room and all cramp,
It's raining now and I feel damp.

Many times we pass the burning light,
And the glowing circle,
Soon to end our flight,
Land is in sight,
We have ended our flight.

Rosie Nicholl (12)
Monmouth Comprehensive School

MY JOURNEY

A journey that goes long and far,
Makes you feel as bright as a star,
Or gloomy, like at 2 o'clock in the morning,
These emotions change without warning,
The highs and lows - just go with the flow.
Who cares? Not me - not anyone I know.
It's my life, not yours!

The shouting from my mother
Causes a bit of a bother,
It's because she cares and worries so.
These are the things that I've come to know,
These are the times we show our love,
(Though not always as peaceful as a dove),
It makes me a part of my family.

Our love is never-ending,
It shines just like the sun,
Although at times the sun goes in
And the moonlight then does come.
That's when I dream, and when I wake,
The darkness goes to hide,
But it matters not, for I'm certain that
There's always light on the other side.

Chris Davies (12)
Monmouth Comprehensive School

MIND OF A MURDERER

A small, chocolate-brown mouse nibbling endlessly at
a piece of mouldy cheese.

A pound coin jingling and jangling in someone's pocket
crying out to be spent on a jam doughnut.

The tall imposing statue of Big Ben chiming out in to
the ice-cold morning air like a warrior without fear.

A gigantic dinosaur savagely tearing someone's head
off like the savage beast he is.

The huge force of an almighty avalanche tearing
down the hills onto a sleepy town like white death.

A tall tree shaking helplessly in the strong and deadly
winter gales of the fir covered mountain.

An out of control lorry swerving from side to side
uncontrollably driven by a fearless madman.

Tom Probert (13)
Monmouth Comprehensive School

THE SURPRISE

I lay in my bed,
A smart grin across my face.
I knew the surprise they were planning,
That's why I'd already packed my case.

They had a surprise holiday booked,
Somewhere cool and exotic I hoped,
They didn't know that I knew,
Hiding this secret, I don't know how I coped.

When Mum came bouncing into my room,
I tried to act surprised and cool.
She said, 'Pack your things we need to go.'
I couldn't wait to jump in the pool.

At the end of the day we were ready to go,
We got in the car,
And drove off to Heathrow!

Lauren Homer (13)
Monmouth Comprehensive School

A PLACE IN MY HEART

The bag sat in front of me, still and non-moving,
Suddenly coming to life, unveiling things
That I never knew meant so much!

Surprises spilling out from a desert island,
Here I seek my freedom and solitude.

A pink shell that lies on the bottom of the ocean,
It has taken a place in my heart.

The life of my enemies, trapped in glass bottles,
Hammering and pounding, trying to get out.

Confidence that I never knew I had,
Boiling and spilling over the bag.

The people I love and admire in a book of photos,
Staring out at me from every gold leafed page.

I can make myself heard using this microphone,
Making my voice rise above the crowd.

Natasha Richardson (14)
Monmouth Comprehensive School

NEXT TO ME!

When you're next to me
I can feel your warm breath down my neck,
It sends shivers down my spine
Knowing you're next to me,
Knowing you're watching, listening to my every move.
As you slide and glide past me as I walk in the dark
I feel a quick brush of hair across my face,
It makes me run, run as far away as I can,
But it doesn't matter how much I run
Or how fast I run you're always there
Watching, listening, waiting
For the right moment to make yourself known.
I don't know who you are or why you are waiting
I just know you're part of me now,
And however hard I try you will always be there.

Laura Wells (13)
Monmouth Comprehensive School

LONELINESS

As he walks down
Looking at the sunset,
Holding hands with the air
He looks at the other people
Holding hands with someone else.

As he sits in the restaurant
Watching the waitress walk by
Without noticing him,
He looks at the other people
Ordering their food.

As he sits in the back of the cinema
Watching the people kissing,
Feeling lonely
He looks at the people who pass,
But they don't look at him.

Hannah Davies (13)
Monmouth Comprehensive School

THE KILLER

Eagle, eagle flying high,
Calling out a hungry cry.
Gripping thermals in the sky
Wondering where the next meal will lie.

On the ground far below
Creatures scurry to and fro.
Rabbits grazing in the sun,
Baby rabbits having fun.

Unaware what's going on,
Up above the hunt's begun.
Sweeping, swooping, coming down,
Coming closer to the ground.

Talons poised ready to grip,
Run, panic, quick, quick, quick.
Swoop, screech, snap, cry,
Dust and fur begin to fly.

Is the meal in his grip
Or is the rabbit just too quick?
The dust has settled, the prey's escaped,
The hungry bird will have to wait.

Sophie Grice (11)
Monmouth Comprehensive School

THE INVISIBLE MAN

The sparkling studded necklace
was worn by a queen,

Shakespeare used this feather
when he wrote his first play,

these boots helped win England
the 1966 World Cup,

when it comes to dusk
the invisible man appears,

I constructed
all of these memories,

the enchanting voice
was that of a king,

all of these imaginings vanished
when I closed the bag.

Joel Price (13)
Monmouth Comprehensive School

JOURNEYS

J   ust another twenty miles to go, please!
O   ver tired children, feeling sick.
U   nder stress parents praying for peace.
R   ed-hot sun irritating the kids.
N   ever enough room in the back.
E   yes feeling heavy,
Y   awning and falling asleep.
S   topping to go to a hotel for a good night's sleep.

Michael Chandler (12)
Monmouth Comprehensive School

THE CHILD IN ME

My mother shows me pictures, and tells me
This is you aged two, or five, or eight.
I don't believe her.
The face from the photos is vibrant,
Clear-eyed and smiling.
How can I connect that with the face
In the mirror, bulbous and swollen,
Thick-lipped and punctured with spots,
Visibly marked by the passage of adolescence.
The form in the pictures, graceful and delicate,
Could never have contorted into my ungainly frame,
Wrapped in thick swathes of flesh, bulging
And spreading out from under its disguise of heavy cloth.
How could those soft, raven waves have become
The dull unmanageable wires that sprout from my head?
Those nimble fingers my clumsy, hopeless paws?
And yet my mother insists that this was I,
Ensnaring my dad in the conspiracy.
So, to please her, I make non-committal noises,
Stare into the mirror trying to see
If any of that child remains in me.

Nicola Gooch (17)
Monmouth Comprehensive School

THE SPACEMAN

The spaceman puts on his special furry shoes,
He cannot see so he puts on his light,
Then walks down the bumpy slope,
It is there in front of him,
He reaches out to grab the chocolate gateau.

Chris Toner (12)
Monmouth Comprehensive School

THE CRY OF THE CATS!

Moonlight,
Darkness all around,
In the bushes, under cars, that's where they will be,
'Miaow' the cats say to each other.

Cats, cats they are everywhere,
They're there all night long!

Cats, cats all about,
Screeching, preaching,
Purring,
Till the sight of dawn.

Darkness disappeared,
This happens all night long!

Katie Sholl (11)
Monmouth Comprehensive School

IN MY LIFE!

In my life I have learnt many things
Like maths and science, and playing the strings.
In my life I've learnt to read,
To count, write and plant a seed.
Another thing is I love to dance,
Maybe when I'm older I'll have a chance.
Me and my friends have lots of fun,
We're always shining in the sun.
I love my mum and I love my dad,
We're so happy, I'm never sad.
But the most important thing of all is me,
I think I've turned out just right as you can see!

Bethan Powell (12)
Monmouth Comprehensive School

BACK TO RECEPTION

Bending down to reach my coat peg
I nearly lose my balance and fall over.
I pull up my white cotton socks and rush towards the teacher
Automatically sitting cross-legged on the floor with my hands
folded in my lap.
'Zips on lips! Zips on lips!' exclaims the teacher.
'Emma; in *ring-a-ring o' roses*, what do you have a pocket full of?'
We rush over to our overstuffed trays,
A herd of elephants.
My palms sweat under the waxy Crayola trademark
As I aimlessly scrawl on paper
Out come beads, strings, puzzles and plasticine,
'I can count to three!'
A pocket full of . . . daisies?
Crouching on foot-high chairs at two-foot high tables
Queuing for lukewarm milk with one thin, blue straw
To sickly slide and dribble down our throats.
The bell rings for break time.
'You can't play tag with us.'
Hands on heads to wait for quiet.
'If you let me play you can come to my party.'
A pocket full of . . . noses?
Grazed knees and tangled legs
As the skipping rope towers above our heads.
Back inside we cuddle the teacher for her special toy of the day,
Listening to its story like attentive, devoted, loyal puppy dogs
Systematically washing our hands for lunch
Standing in a straight line with our lunch boxes held in two hands
Saying our 'Thank you for our daily bread' prayer.
Can we swap our sandwiches?
Posies.

Emma Garlick (16)
Monmouth Comprehensive School

A WELSH MISUNDERSTANDING

My cousin John who lives in Manchester
And wants to be a doctor,
Says that everyone who lives in Wales
Lives on the top of a mountain in terrible weather,
And keeps lots of sheep on farms,
And grows daffodils in the garden
And eats leeks every day
And sings out of tune in choir.

I say to my cousin John that he is wrong.
The only person he knows that lives in Wales is me.
We do grow daffodils in the garden,
But I live in Raglan, not on top of a mountain,
And the sun does shine sometimes
And I don't keep sheep,
And I prefer chicken nuggets to leeks
And I certainly don't sing out of tune.

My cousin John who lives in Manchester
Says that I am in a bit of a muddle.
If I don't do any of those things, I can't be Welsh;
And everybody in Raglan is also in a bit of a muddle
Because they live so near England.
But he says that, anyway, he does like Wales
Because it reminds him of dragons.

I say to my cousin John that he is wrong
He is the one that's in a muddle.
I know very well that I am Welsh
And so do all my friends in Raglan
And I have never seen a dragon in Wales.
But I say that, anyway, I like muddle
Because it reminds me of John's room.

Rhydian Avent (11)
Monmouth Comprehensive School

IT HAPPENED ON A BUS

It happened on a bus I'm sure,
One or two decks, maybe more . . .
Did someone shave? Did someone shout?
What was all the fuss about?
Was there a dog with muddy feet,
Or did a Martian share your seat?

This extraordinary thing happens twice a year,
Everyone who goes on the bus, comes off in great fear.
It started in 1953,
When someone shouted, 'I need a wee.'
He said, 'Give me a loo, give me a potty,
Give me the potty or I'll go dotty.'

I suppose you're wondering why people are in fear,
Well it happened the very next year.
When someone shouted with glee,
'I really need a wee.'
If people don't go to the potty,
They start to go dotty.

The person started to swell,
He looked like a rusty old bell.
The poor man started to expand,
He stretched just like an elastic band.
The poor old soul exploded,
People thought he had been loaded.

So now you've been warned about bus number fifty-three,
You know what to do if you need a wee
If you happen to be on that bus . . .
Please don't make a *fuss*.

Have a nice day!

Kirsty Usher (11)
Monmouth Comprehensive School

FOOTBALL

Got to wake up, get nice and clean,
It's the start of the young footballers' scene.
It's Sunday morning, the sun is beaming,
Got to get there and stop dreaming.
Mums and dads on the line,
The grass is damp but very fine.
The players walk on the pitch
Admiring the season's new kit.

The whistle blows,
The linesman's flags fly,
The opening kick
Goes high into the sky.

The forwards run,
The defenders mark,
A pass is sent
Across the green park.

People scream and shout
To pass the ball and move it out.

As the final whistle blows
The players shake hands
As the manager reviews his pre-match plans.
'We've won,' they shout,
And race around.
More training on Friday at our home ground!

Jonathan Willington (11)
Monmouth Comprehensive School

THE LIFE OF A WATERFALL

I stand here looking at a wall
Of water from a waterfall,
It falls down with a sounding splash,
Hitting the bottom with a noisy crash.

The water drops from out of the sky
To meet the river up so high.
It falls to Earth in the form of rain,
And along a river it needs to drain.

Along its course the river does wind,
For its destination it needs to find.
It flows along at ferocious speeds,
Through riverbanks adorned with reeds.

Sometimes the water just drifts along,
For via this course it can't go wrong.
Until it nears the journey's end,
It travels round that final bend.

It gathers speed right up to the edge
Of the hillside's final inviting ledge.
It eventually tips over the side,
On the final leg of its ride.

Through this barrage that's a wall
Of water from a waterfall.
It's finally come here to splash
With a thunderous, noisy, deafening crash.

Alouisia Jones (11)
Monmouth Comprehensive School

THE SEARCH FOR MY PARENTS

Slippery, sliding, soft sand lying on the beach,
I'm wading quietly through the sand,
My bare feet feeling the hardness of the wet sand.

I get down on my knees,
My hands are wet,
I feel light-headed, the tide's coming in.
I'm dizzy . . . falling . . . thud.

'Hello . . . hello . . . she's unconscious.'
A stranger is leaning over,
I jump up. 'I'm not, I'm soaking wet.'
My hands tingle.

With my last ounce of strength I scramble up a sandbank,
Wind is gale force, I'm getting blown down,
My cold hands grab something and I pull myself up.

More sand blows, it's in my eyes, I'm at the top,
Bugs scurry round,
It's cold, I pass out, suddenly I'm on a desert island.

I wake up . . . my parents have gone,
It's dark, I get up and lose my footing, I fall down,
At the bottom of the hill is the sea, the tide's fully in.

I stand up, I fall back down, my legs are like jelly,
My feet hurt . . . my hands are cold,
I can't see . . . I've gone deaf.

I can't smell anything . . . I can't breathe . . . I can't breathe.
My parents are coming, I'm following them into the light.

Stephanie Barclay (12)
Monmouth Comprehensive School

THE JOURNEY

Have you ever had that fear?
The feeling of sick dread,
That thought that tomorrow you might as well be dead.
The pressing of cold, clammy bodies
Against your sickly white skin.
The jolting of the floor, on your journey to that place.
And the hundreds of Jewish prayers,
Whispered, like a breath on the wind.

There's no stopping on this journey,
And nothing ever changes
Except the light filtering through those gaps.
It's hard to keep up hope,
That candle of life is flickering,
The clock never stops ticking.
But yet, there are still those Jewish prayers,
Whispered, like a breath on the wind.

The screeching of a silent enemy,
We don't have to ask, it's so easy to guess.
The doors opened, I am blinded,
Yet I don't need to see,
But only feel, the misery of this place.
As I stumble through the mud,
My ears can't stop hearing those Jewish prayers,
Whispered, in this concentration camp.

The journey of my body has come to an abrupt end,
But my emotions will never stop, stop on their journey.
I feel terror every step of my journey through life.
But those Jewish prayers don't stop,
That loving whisper, like a breath on the wind.

Emma Buckels (12)
Monmouth Comprehensive School